Also by Michael Holzman

Lukács's Road to God
Writing as Social Action (with Marilyn Cooper)
James Jesus Angleton: The C.I.A., and the Craft of
Counterintelligence
Pax 1934-1941 (novel)
Guy Burgess: Revolutionary in an Old School Tie
The Black Poverty Cycle and How to End It
Minority Students and Public Education:
A Resource Book (Two Volumes)
Donald and Melinda Maclean: Idealism and Espionage
The Chains of Black America
The Language of Anti-Communism

..

THREE-FIFTHS OF AN EDUCATION

How the Schools Do Not Educate African-Americans

Chelmsford Press   Briarcliff Manor, New York

...

Chelmsford Press   Briarcliff Manor, New York

ISBN-13: 978-0692964002
ISBN-10: 0692964002

For Jane

Acknowledgments

I would like to thank Rosa A. Smith, RiShawn Biddle, Phillip Jackson, Eric Cooper, Dana Brown, the Bureau of the Census and the National Center for Education Statistics.

Errors are, of course, my own. I would be grateful to have them brought to my attention so that they might be corrected.

THREE-FIFTHS OF AN EDUCATION

How the Schools Do Not Educate African-Americans

Michael Holzman

Table of Contents

Introduction

This is where you might expect to find a case study of racial discrimination or a story about a child who could have had a satisfying, contributory, life, but was frustrated by racism. Or, perhaps, a story about a teacher, who, against all the odds . . . Or an "inner city" school principal, who, using her own money . . .

But we are all adults here. The facts should suffice. They should more than suffice.

There has been a persistent theme in the media, explicitly, and in scholarly studies, implicitly, that economic class is much more important than race for the analysis of American society. This is, of course, a Marxist position, one clung to by the Communist Party of the United States to its dying day. But the basis of American society, as even some Communists admitted, is what W. E. B. Du Bois called the Color Line: racism. This was embodied in the original wording of the Constitution with its three-fifths rule for counting enslaved Africans and their descendants:

> Representatives and direct Taxes shall be apportioned among the several States which may be included within this Union, according to their respective Numbers, which shall be determined by adding to the whole Number of free Persons, including those bound to Service for a Term of Years, and excluding Indians not taxed, three fifths of all other Persons.[1]

"Those bound to Service for a Term of Years" were presumably White indentured servants. Everyone knew that the descendants of enslaved Africans were those referred to as "all other Persons." The question of race-based slavery later dominated debates in the Senate until the imposition of the "gag" rule by southern senators barred its discussion. The color line, as Jim Crow, determined social structures and social relations in much of the country until the 1970s. Even then, despite *Brown v. Board of Education*, the Voting Rights Act and similar legislation, *de facto* Jim Crow did not vanish; it was transformed into "Jim Crow by another name," primarily through the operations of schools and prisons. Today, the stronghold of what Michelle Alexander branded as "The New Jim Crow" is found in the states of the former Confederacy, running from Virginia to Texas, with satellites in various urban centers, some southern, some not, especially in the line from Louisville, Kentucky to Milwaukee, Wisconsin, but also in such cities as Chicago, Cleveland, Detroit, Philadelphia, Baltimore, Washington, D.C. and New York City.

Racism is not merely what its nineteenth-century founders called "thinking in terms of races." It is the classification of certain people, certain groups, as less than equal to those in the dominant group. In the United States this means that those people perceived as the descendants of enslaved Africans have their lives restricted—literally as well as figuratively—by the actions of individuals, acting as individuals, which one might call petty racism—and by the actions of individuals acting in an official capacity: federal, state and local officials, prosecutors and judges, members of boards of education, employers and teachers. This latter is state-sponsored racism, which is sometimes called "structural racism," a label, however, that avoids the personal responsibility of those controlling the operations of the institutions in question.

There are now about 21 million descendants of enslaved Africans living in the former slave states, slightly more than half of the total African-American population of the country. On average, a quarter of the residents of those states are African-Americans, a proportion varying from twelve percent in Texas to 37% in Mississippi; a population that remains, to a large extent, rural. There is another group of states with large African-American populations: California, Illinois, Michigan, New Jersey, New York, Ohio and Pennsylvania, together including 14% of the national population of descendants of enslaved Africans. The proportion of the nearly thirteen million African-Americans in these states varies from 7% of the total in California (which is, nonetheless, three million) to 15% in New York (also approximately three million). In these states the African-American population, descended from the participants in the Great Migration, is largely urban.

Texas is an outlier in its racial and ethnic population distribution among the former slave states, its 3.3 million African-Americans vastly outnumbered by the ten million Hispanics, who, with the twenty million White, non-Hispanics, dominate the state's demographics. California, with its similarly large Hispanic population, is the outlier in the second group, with a socio-economic situation for African-Americans similar to that of Texas.[2] Hispanic-Americans, except in New Mexico and parts of Colorado, where their settlements date from before those areas became part of the United States, can be viewed as a fairly traditional recent immigrant group. Their socio-economic trajectory is similar to that of Italians in the early twentieth-century, Jews before them and the Irish after the Famine: the first generation struggling with the language and mores of their new country, the second becoming acculturated and the third forgetting that history of assimilation. As is traditional with the first generation of immigrants, the twenty million first-generation Hispanic Americans, where numerous, are relegated to the lowest paid work, the least desirable neighborhoods, the worst schools. Elsewhere, despite their centuries of residence in this country, those are the places allocated to the descendants of enslaved Africans.

The Founders were remarkably prescient with their calculation of the "three-fifths" rule. Even today the descendants of enslaved Africans in many ways count only as something like three-fifths of the White residents of this country. The average family income of African-Americans in the former slave states, $46,000, is approximately three-fifths of the median White family income in those states. The Black unemployment rate is twice that of the White unemployment rate, as is the poverty rate.[*] The three-fifths rule applies to the other group of states with large African-American populations as well. Black family incomes in those states are also three-fifths of White family incomes; their unemployment rate for African-Americans is two and a half times that for White, non-Hispanics; the Black poverty rate is more than twice as high as that of their White neighbors. Given that these two groups of states taken

---

[*] These data categories, here and elsewhere in this book, are from the U.S. Census, accessible at census.gov.

7

together include 33 million of the nation's 41 million descendants of enslaved Africans, it is unsurprising that the national data as well follows the three-fifths rule. Thus, nationally, the African-American median family income is three-fifths of White median family income; the Black employment and poverty rates double those of White Americans. The consequences of these disparities are obvious. African-Americans are, in effect, a distinct and underprivileged caste within American society, not because of the activities or characters of individual African-Americans, but because they are recognizably descendants of enslaved Africans and the racist actions by other individuals and groups that incurs.

The American education system is an important mechanism that maintains and perpetuates this situation. In the United States today, education (along with inheritance) determines economic status. In 2015, full-time workers between the ages of 25 and 34 who had not completed high school had incomes averaging $25,000 per year, while those with Master's degrees or higher averaged $60,000.[3] Among White young adults, the wage span runs from $30,000 for those who had not completed high school to $60,000 for those with a Master's degree or higher. Black young adults who have not completed high school have annual incomes not greatly different from their White peers, $29,000, but their higher education premium is much less, reaching only $54,000 for those with Master's degrees or higher. White young adults reach the national median income by earning a two-year, Associate's degree, while it requires the completion of college, a Bachelor's degree, for Black young adults to reach the national median income for their age group. Black earnings for workers with less than a high school diploma are 90% of those of White earners. Above that, they average just over 80%.[†]

That difference could be called the racial penalty.

[†] Nationally, in 2015 median usual weekly earnings of full-time wage and salary workers was $920 to White workers and $680 for Black. White women were, on average, paid 81% of White male earnings; Black women were paid 90% of Black male earnings (Bureau of Labor Statistics, Report 1062, September 2016, table 16).

Income by Educational Attainment and Race		
	White	Black
Less than High School Diploma	$498	$448
High School Graduate	$706	$578
Some college, no degree	$767	$619
Associate's Degree	$826	$681
Bachelor's Degree and higher	$1,245	$1,010

Median usual weekly earnings of full-time wage and salary workers, 2015 averages. (Bureau of Labor Statistics, Report 1062, September 2016, table 17.)

Educational attainment is often figured as a "ladder" for socio-economic mobility, but education itself follows the three-fifths rule. While, nationally, 32% of White American adults have attained a Bachelor's degree or higher, only 20% of African-American adults have had an education bringing them to that level. And while 15% of African-Americans adults have not completed high school, this truncated education was incurred by only 11% of White, non-Hispanic, Americans. The former slave states and some of the northern urban areas show more extreme outcomes. Unsurprisingly, the most extreme are Louisiana, Mississippi and South Carolina, where between a fifth and a quarter of African-American adults do not have high school diplomas (or the equivalent) and only 15% (or fewer) have four-year college degrees. This is less than 60% (three-fifths) of White educational attainment in Louisiana and Mississippi and less than half of White educational attainment in South Carolina. In the north, New York State has a higher proportion of African-American residents without high school diplomas than the former slave state average. Michigan, Pennsylvania and Ohio support Bachelor's degree attainment for their Black adults at levels below the average of the former slave states and all the states in their group, other than California, have racial disparities in college education in line with the three-fifths rule.

The economic effect of this is clear: lower educational attainment means lower-incomes, with all that implies for the quality of life, mortality rates and opportunities for the next generation.

There are two obvious questions about such a state of affairs: Who benefits? Who is responsible?

9

Three-Fifths of an Education

It is not clear that any particular group benefits *economically* today from discrimination against the descendants of enslaved Africans, as the slave masters, plantation and factory owners once benefitted from the surplus value of the labor of their enslaved ancestors. There are now immigrants, especially Hispanic immigrants, available for the least attractive, lowest paid, most dangerous work, with threats of deportation taking the place of the overseer's whip. And, increasingly, there are robots. Indeed, the unemployment rates of African-Americans—two or three times those of White Americans—may indicate the superfluity of their labor under what is sometimes called advanced capitalism. More than half a century ago the University of Chicago economist Gary Becker "made a central observation: discrimination has consequences for people being discriminated against, as well as for the people engaged in it.

> If discrimination depresses the wages of black workers relative to those of similarly qualified whites, a discriminator who, say, does not want to hire black staff will have to pay more to hire white employees. This creates two costs: the black worker is paid less, and the discriminating employer incurs greater expense to obtain the same productivity.[4]

Seen through the lens of the Chicago school of economics, this might seem paradoxical. Why would rational agents voluntarily incur costs by practicing discrimination? First, there are some matters that run counter to Becker's analysis. We have seen recently that the operations of the new Jim Crow such as the "red-lining" practiced by banks can produce considerable profits from higher interest rates and foreclosures. And as W. E. B. Du Bois pointed out long ago, not all costs, and not all profits, are monetary. There are, for example, the benefits of racial prejudice itself for populist politicians and their paymasters, allowing them to generate the false consciousness necessary for their success among the impoverished White voters of their constituencies. These things, along with minor issues, such as employment opportunities for White police and prison guards, and deeply engrained racism itself, suffice to keep the system of racial discrimination in place.

Who is responsible may be a more fraught question. It is no longer acceptable to blame Black people themselves. The "crisis of the Negro family" and drugs in the ghetto and such are now the common problems of what used to be the White American working class; epidemics of "opioids" replacing "crack" (which replaced heroin) devastating rural families as much as urban, and divorce rates of White marriages exceeding the nightmare levels identified by Daniel Patrick Moynihan in his diagnosis of the supposed characteristic ills of the Black family in his time. A comforting answer is structural racism, as if structures by themselves had motivations and agency. Corporations may be people, for the purposes of those standing to profit from that definition, but there is—as yet—no argument that governmental institutions are themselves people. Federal agencies, state and local governments, boards of education, colleges and schools do not haunt our streets like bureaucratic ectoplasm. The actions of each are determined by individuals and it is individuals who are responsible, their actions and their inaction; those who commit these evils and those who could prevent them and do not.

*   *   *

The following pages focus on the effects on African-American children of the presently constituted public education system, beginning with a description of a school system that does not practice racial discrimination, followed by a national overview and then moving on to states and cities with large Black populations.‡ While the facts on the ground, as it were, are laid out, an attempt will be made to identify how people in decision-making roles might make other decisions than those that they habitually do make today, so that, someday, the descendants of those enslaved Africans who

---

‡ Public schools are the primary focus, as 90% of American children attend public schools and as public schools express the nature of our society. This does not mean that private schools—religious and independent—are in general less racist in operation. Perhaps, in many cases, the opposite. Therefore some attention is paid to them here as well.

11

Three-Fifths of an Education

survived enslavement, the middle passage and slavery itself, may no longer be treated as worth just three-fifths of the value of other Americans.

Notes

[1] Article 1, Section 2, Paragraph 3 of the United States Constitution.

[2] In both of these states median family income for Black residents is 71% of White and the poverty rates less than each group of states' average.

[3] U.S. Department of Education, Digest of Education Statistics, 2016, Table 502.30. Median annual earnings of full-time year-round workers 25 to 34 years old and full-time year-round workers as a percentage of the labor force, by sex, race/ethnicity, and educational attainment: Selected years, 1995 through 2015

[4] Murphy, Kevin M. "How Gary Becker saw the scourge of discrimination." Chicago Book Review, June 15, 2015. http://review.chicagobooth.edu/magazine/winter-2014/how-gary-becker-saw-the-scourge-of-discrimination.

A School System With Equal Educational Opportunities

We need not rely on thought experiments in order to visualize a more equitable system of education in the United States. There is the school system managed by the Department of Defense. The Department of Defense operates a global prekindergarten to twelfth grade education system serving over 73,000 students. It is, in effect, the nation's 45th largest school district. Since President Truman ordered the desegregation of the military, the nation's armed forces have progressed from being one of the most segregated to being one of the best-integrated areas of American society. This is not to say that there are not racists in the military, there are, of course, but the intolerance for over racist actions in the armed forces is exemplary for the rest of our society and has a profound effect on educational opportunities for the children of African-American military families.

There are 1.3 million active duty military personal, of whom 17% are Black or African-American, a slightly larger percentage than in the general population. Nineteen percent (206,227) of enlisted personnel are Black as are 9% (21,921) of officers (2014).[1] We can assume, then, that by and large, decisions in the military, including decisions about the schools of the Department of Defense, are most likely to be taken by White, non-Hispanics. Very few (less than 1%) of military personnel are without a high school diploma or GED. Ninety-two percent of enlisted personnel have a high school diploma or equivalent; 6% have Bachelor's degrees; 1% have more advanced educations. Among officers, the distribution of educational attainment is reversed: 7% officers have only a high school diploma or equivalent; 43% have Bachelor's degrees and 41% have more advanced educational qualifications.

More than a third (38%) of military personnel are married with children, while just 6% are single with children. The approximate average annual income of enlisted personnel is $40,400, that of

15

officers $81,000, which gives an average annual income for African-American military personnel of $44,300. In sum, the typical African-American member of the military is more likely to have completed secondary school, but less likely to have postsecondary degrees, has a higher individual income and if a parent is more likely to be married than a member of the general African-American population.

Black or African-American		
	Military	**US**
No HS/GED	1%	15%
HS/GED	84%	64%
BA	10%	13%
Advanced	5%	8%
Average Individual Income	$44,300	$39,400[2]
Average Family Income	$47,000[3]	$47,000
Single with Children	6%	16%

If we look at National Assessment of Educational Progress (NAEP) results for the key eighth grade reading indicator, we see that over-all, the Department of Defense schools outcomes are considerably better than those for public schools in general, with less than half the percentage of students at the Below Basic level and 50% more at the proficient level.

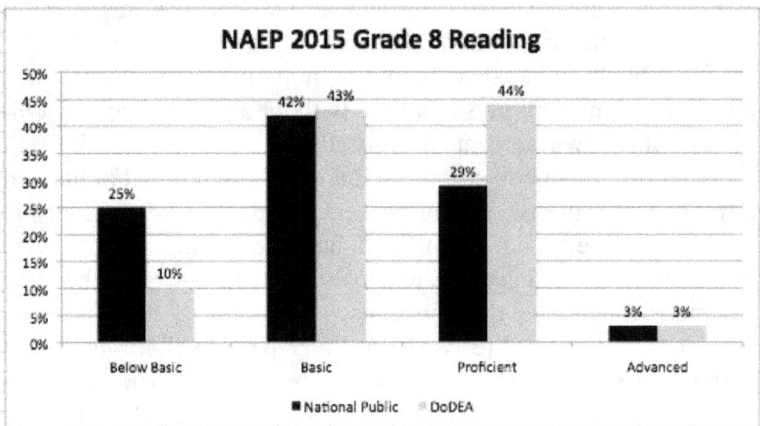

NAEP 2015 Grade 8 Reading

Disaggregating these results by race, we see that among White, non-Hispanic, students, the Department of   Defense schools again have better, if less dramatic, out-comes.

NAEP 2015 Grade 8 Reading

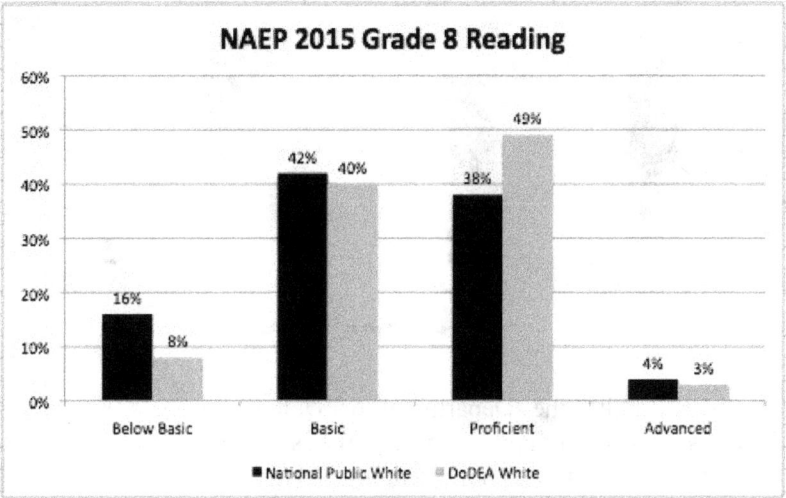

However, the picture for Black students *is* dramatic, with less than a quarter of those who in the general population test at the Below Basic level, between two and three times as many at the proficient level.

Three-Fifths of an Education

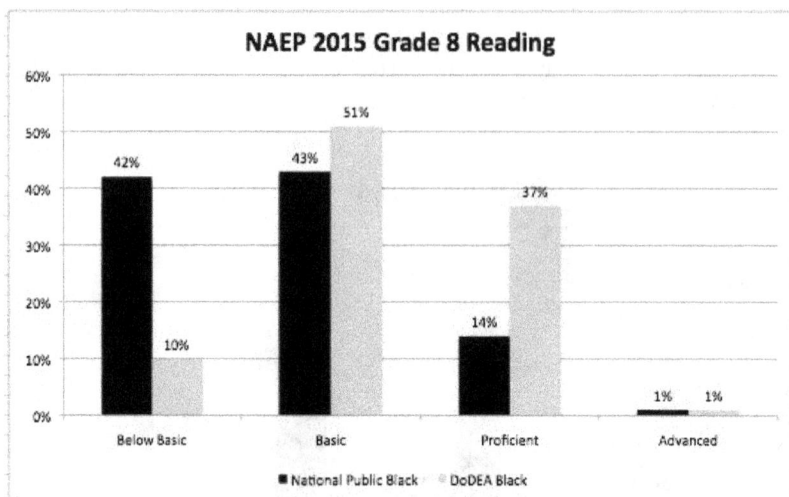

NAEP 2015 Grade 8 Reading

Interestingly, the Department of Defense schools results for Black students are approximately the same as those for White students in the nation's public schools.

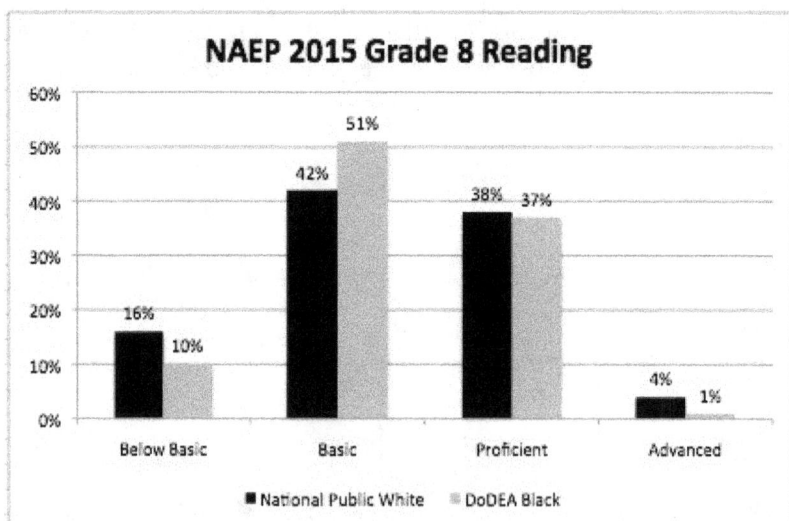

NAEP 2015 Grade 8 Reading

The overall difference, then, between the outcomes for eighth grade reading between the Department of Defense schools and the nation's public schools in general is the strikingly superior performance of the Department of Defense schools in regard to their Black students. To what should this be attributed? If we look back at our comparison table, there does not seem to be an obvious causal factor:

Black or African-American		
	Military	US
No HS/GED	1%	15%
HS/GED	84%	64%
BA	10%	13%
Advanced	5%	8%
Average Individual Income	$44,300	$39,400[4]
Average Family Income	$47,000[5]	$47,000
Single with children	6%	16%

Parental education differences are pretty much a wash: Black military families are less likely to have quit school before receiving a diploma, but also less likely to have a Bachelor's degree or above. African-American military personnel have higher individual incomes and slightly higher family incomes than the general African-American population (perhaps because all are, by definition, employed). However, while Black students in Department of Defense schools score at the proficient or above level 38% of the time, Black students ineligible for the National Lunch Program (that is, with middle class incomes) in all national public schools do so just 26% of the time, therefore family income explains only part of the difference. And nineteen percent of Black students, nationally, who respond to NAEP indicating that they live in home with a father, are at the proficient or above level, compared to 12% who give no response. (This is less of a difference than that for White, non-Hispanic, students, where the percentages are 46% and 32%.) As this probably correlates with income, again it does not seem to explain

19

the difference between the outcomes of Department of Defense and other public schools.

This leaves us with what is usually called "school culture." In other words, it is probable that the Department of Defense schools partake of the general, official, anti-racist culture of the military. They give Black and White students equal educational opportunities, equal access to educational resources, and given those, race ceases to be a determining factor in educational achievement.

The schools of the Department of Defense show what can be done. Let us now look at what is in fact done in other American schools.

The National Picture

The promise of the United States of America, what Gunnar Myrdal called "the American Creed," includes equal protection under the laws; freedom of belief, speech, and association; and equal opportunity. The promise of equal opportunity takes many forms, one of the most important is equal opportunity for a good education. There is an alchemy in modern society by virtue of which accumulated material objects—money, say, or property—can be converted into the less tangible form of culture, most fundamentally, education, and vice versa. For those with little or no material riches, education is a Philosopher's Stone, capable of transforming limited, restricted, impoverished lives into the opportunity for full social, cultural and economic participation in American society. For the descendants of enslaved Africans education offers the hope of a transformation from lives many of which are lived at a scale three-fifths of those of others, to lives embodying that equal opportunity promised to other American citizens by the Founders.

Those are promises and hopes. What is the reality?

The U.S. Department of Education's National Assessment of Educational Progress is generally accepted as an objective measure of student skills and subject area knowledge. The assessments are given to carefully structured random samples of students at grades 4, 8 and 12 for both public and private schools in twelve areas: Civics, Economics, Geography, Mathematics, Music, Reading, Science, Technology and Engineering Literacy, U.S. History, Visual Arts, Vocabulary and Writing. (Not all of these are used in each of the alternate years the assessments are administered.) NAEP provides results by such categories as race and ethnicity, gender, eligibility for the National Lunch Program (a measure of family income with the dividing line at approximately $45,000), school type and location and many more. NAEP can tell us how successful the American education system has been in providing students with the knowledge and the skills they need—the components of that Philosopher's Stone—for a full adult life.

The following section compares national outcomes in selected areas for all students and specifically for White and Black students, both those eligible for the National Lunch Program and those Ineligible.[6] We will begin with the two key basic skills: reading and mathematics. Reading first.

NAEP Reading Assessments

How well do American schools teach children to read? On average, something more than a third of students, without regard to race, ethnicity, gender, income or whether they attend public or private schools, read at grade level in grades 4 and 8 (NAEP calls this "proficient or above"), while a third of the students in fourth grade and more than a quarter in eighth grade test at "Below Basic."[§] All in all, the line between NAEP's Below Basic classification and illiteracy is difficult to discern. All of these figures had improved in parallel between 1992, the first year for which NAEP now provides data, and 2015. Or to put that another way, over the past quarter of a century the nation's primary school students have shown a general improvement in the essential skill of reading. Middle school students have shown similar improvements in their reading ability over that period. However, the percentage of fourth graders reading at grade level was nearly the same as that of eighth graders in both years. Four more years of schooling have had little effect on the relative reading skills of students (except at the lowest category): nearly two-thirds cannot read well; nearly one-third of fourth graders and one quarter of eighth graders have difficulty reading at all.

[§] Although the National Assessment of Educational Progress does not define "Below Basic," we can deduce from other NAEP definitions that eighth-grade students at that level are unable to "locate information; identify statements of main idea, theme, or author's purpose" or "make simple inferences from texts." They cannot be expected to be able to interpret the meaning of a word as it is used in the text or "be able to state judgments and give some support about content and presentation of content."

NAEP Reading: All Students				
Level	Fourth Grade		Eighth Grade	
	1992	2015	1992	2013
Proficient or Above	28%	36%	29%	35%
Below Basic	38%	31%	31%	24%

Black and White Student Achievement: Reading

We are so accustomed to the "three-fifths" status of descendants of enslaved Africans in this country that many people accept without question that there will be racial differences in, say, reading achievement among elementary and secondary school students. But why should that be the case? Some people believe in differences of ability between what are called races in the United States. This belief is complicated by matters of fact—the evidence put forth for differences of ability is hardly convincing—and by definitional issues. The usual racial categories, such as those used by NAEP, are White, Black, Asian, American Indian and Hispanic (the last of these including people who can belong to any of the other categories). These are, of course, scientifically nonsensical. For example, some people now think of themselves, or are thought of, as White, often enough as a negative, residual category: not Black, Asian or Hispanic. This is a profound change from the era when White was a partly class-based category, so that a British general might express surprise that private soldiers had white skin and Italian peasants were no more considered White than, say, Polish Jews. In the United States slave owners (we think here, for example, of Thomas Jefferson) interbred with their African slaves, and their descendants, and since Emancipation sexual relations (and their consequences) between people perceived as White and people perceived as Black have no doubt continued. The category of "Asian" is, if possible, even more irrational. Han Chinese have no more to do, genetically, with Tamil citizens of India than Afghans with either. And all that Hispanic residents of the United States have in common is a set of languages, which fewer speak with each generation.

The reason to make these matters explicit is to recover awareness that as "Blackness" is a social and cultural, not a biological,

24

category, differences in educational outcomes are to be traced to social and cultural, not biological, causes, traced to the social and cultural matrix of racism. Or, to put it bluntly, differences in educational outcomes are not natural, they are created by those responsible for the distribution of educational opportunities.

It is, then, not natural, not to be taken for granted, that in 1992, over 90% of Black students were unable to read at grade level in fourth grade and over half in that grade had difficulty reading at all, while one-third of White students were reading at grade level and "just" a quarter had difficulty reading. Nor that by 2015, even though the percentage of Black students reading at grade level had more than doubled, it was still less than half that of White students.

NAEP Reading: Fourth Grade						
Level	Black		White		B/W Gap	
	1992	2015	1992	2015	1992	2015
Proficient or Above	8%	18%	34%	45%	26	27
Below Basic	57%	42%	25%	16%	32	26

There was hardly any difference between fourth and eighth grade in the respective percentages of Black and White students reading at grade level or having difficulty reading in 1992 and 2015. In eighth grade, as in fourth, the gaps between the percentages of Black and White students reading at the proficient or above levels remained basically the same for 23 years.

NAEP Reading: Eighth Grade				
Level	Black		White	
	1992	2015	1992	2015
Proficient or Above	8%	15%	33%	42%
Below Basic	57%	42%	25%	16%

Despite improvements over a generation,[7] at the crucial eighth-grade point in education, an overwhelming majority of America's Black students, 85%, still have not been taught to read at grade level, while nearly half of all White students have been taught to read the books their teachers expect them to read. And nearly half of Black students have difficulty in eighth grade reading at all.[**] Our question, then, is why is it that, in general, schools do not teach Black students to read as well as they teach White students? Perhaps if we go deeper into the data we will find an answer.

Income within Race

If we must make fully conscious our perception of the role of race in defining educational opportunities and outcomes, so we must also not neglect to make fully conscious our perception of the role of family income in determining educational outcomes. As with race, it is not natural that children from lower-income families have lower levels of educational achievement than children from higher income families. It is the result of decisions, official and personal, of those responsible for their education. The fundamental promise of public education is equal opportunity, both as to its nature and its outcomes. When we note differences in educational achievement with reference to family income, as well as race, those differences become a question, not an assumption.

National Lunch Program (NLP) eligibility is NAEP's proxy for income. The program funds free- and reduced-cost school lunches (and sometimes other meals and snacks). *Eligible* students come from lower-income families; *ineligible* students come from more prosperous families, the dividing line being approximately $45,000 in annual income for a family of four. (For comparison, U.S. median family income is $62,400.)[8] Nearly half (47%) of eighth graders from families sufficiently prosperous to make them ineligible for the NLP read at grade level (and only 14% have difficulty reading). On the other hand, just one-fifth (20%) of eighth graders from lower-income (NLP eligible) families read at grade level and more than one-third, 36%, have difficulty reading. Students from families with

---

[**] It is particularly notable, and troubling, that half of *male* Black students have difficulty reading, half of male Black students have been left by their schools virtually illiterate in the context of the increasingly technological American society and economy.

incomes higher than $45,000 per year have more than twice the chance of learning to read as well as their teachers expect than do students from lower-income families. As there are few who believe in an income-based "bell curve" of intelligence, the explanation for these startling differences is most likely differences in educational opportunities, related to family income-based school funding and resource allocation, on the one hand, and educational opportunities outside of school enjoyed by children in higher income families. These differences based on family income are exacerbated for descendants of enslaved Africans by racist operations of schools.

The NLP eligibility dividing line of approximately $45,000 in family income is only slightly lower than the national median family income for Black families, but well below the $73,000 median income for White families. In other words, half of all Black families qualify for the National Lunch Program, as do many more of those Black families with children and an even great proportion of Black families in which there is only one parent present, while a considerably lower proportion of White students in each category are from families whose income qualifies them for free- or reduced-price lunches.

In fourth grade, Black students from families in the upper part of the Black family income distribution read proficiently twice as often as Black students eligible for the National Lunch Program. The effect is similar for White fourth graders. However, this family income benefit is not associated with much of a narrowing of the racial gap. Lower-income fourth grade Black students read less well than lower-income White students and higher income Black fourth graders read less well than higher income White students. On the other hand exactly the same proportion of White students whose family incomes are low enough to make them eligible for free- and reduced-price lunches read as well as Black students from more prosperous families. In other words, in America, in general, race is more important than class when it comes to educational opportunities.

27

NAEP Reading Fourth Grade: Proficient or Above		
Income	Black	White
NLP Eligible (Family income below $45,000)	15%	30%
NLP Ineligible (Family income above $45,000)	30%	54%

If we do not accept that the ability to learn to read is genetically associated with family income, why is it that Black and White students from higher income families are twice as likely to be taught how to read well as Black and White students from lower-income families? If we do not accept that the ability to learn to read is genetically associated with race, why is that White fourth graders from lower-income families are as likely to be taught to read well as Black students from higher income families? Perhaps it is not income per se, but those goods that come with higher incomes: better schools and extra-scholastic educational opportunities (including more highly educated parents). Perhaps it is not race per se, but those goods that are less available for Black students: better schools and extra-scholastic educational opportunities (including more highly educated parents).

That is the situation in fourth grade, the conclusion of lower primary education (and, it happens, where the benefits of high quality pre-school programs appear to tail off.) By eighth grade, students will have spent nine years in school (ten if they went to pre-school). School would have been a very important, if not the most important, influence on their intellectual lives. They would have had hundreds of hours of instruction in basic skills and core curricular content. Looking in the other direction, eighth grade is a pivot point in education. Relative basic skills do not change much from eighth to twelfth grade: those students reading at grade level in eighth grade tend to read at grade level in twelfth grade; those having difficulty reading in eighth grade do not often learn to read better in twelfth grade. At eighth grade, the percentage of students reading at grade level in 2015 was smaller than that in fourth grade for both Black and White students, both those from lower-income and more prosperous families.

NAEP Reading Eighth Grade: Proficient or Above		
Income	Black	White
NLP Eligible (Family income below $45,000)	11%	27%
NLP Ineligible (Family income above $45,000)	26%	50%

By this measure, nearly 90% of Black students from lower-income families and nearly three-quarters of Black students from more prosperous families were not well-prepared for high school graduation, much less for college or careers. Eighth grade achievement levels are a particularly crucial indicator of student learning. In many districts there is a ninth grade "gate" test that determines whether students will be allowed to continue to high school or must repeat a grade. Lack of reading proficiency in eighth grade makes it unlikely that a student will pass such tests. It is at this point that many students decide—or are advised—not to continue their education to or beyond high school graduation.

Family income is a major factor in assessed reading proficiency for both Black and White students. One reason for this is that the quality of the educational opportunities available in this country vary with family income. Another reason is that differences in family income affect or determine out-of-school educational resources. But at issue here for the moment is why three-quarters of even those students from the upper half of the Black family income distribution do not read proficiently at eighth grade. It might be that the higher income educational benefit does not take effect until family incomes reach a point beyond those of most Black families who are not so impoverished as to qualify for the National Lunch Program. Another reason may be that the educational opportunities available in schools attended by Black children do not change, or do not change much, with family income. Under *de facto* segregation, as it now exists in the former Confederate states and in most large cities, schools in predominately Black neighborhoods and communities are less well-resourced than others. A more complicated issue is inter-generational cultural accumulation: the way in which highly educated parents pass down those cultural resources to their children, more or less independently of income. We will now look at that effect.

Parental Education

NAEP asks students to report whether a parent 1) has not completed high school, 2) has graduated, 3) has some education beyond high school or 4) is a college graduate.[††] For every racial/ethnic group classification used by NAEP, additional parental education is associated with increased percentages of students reaching proficiency in grade eight reading.

NAEP Grade Eight Reading: Proficient or Above

[††] It should be borne in mind that these parental educational levels are those reported by the students.

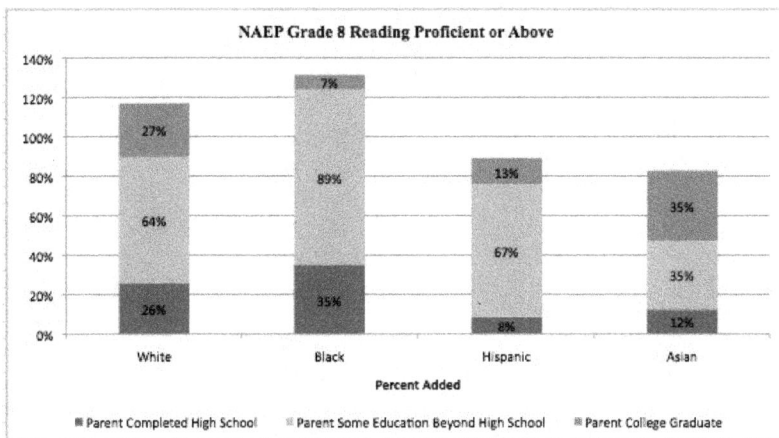

NAEP Grade 8 Reading Proficient or Above

■ Parent Completed High School   ▨ Parent Some Education Beyond High School   ▨ Parent College Graduate

The largest amount of value added from a parental education increment is for Black students who have a parent with some education beyond high school. This 89% increase in the percentage reaching grade level in grade eight reading is great enough to overcome the unusually low increase associated with parental college graduation, bringing the total effect of parental education from high school to college graduation to 131% for Black students.

The higher the educational attainment of adults, the better their children do in school. The better those students do in school, the better their chances of continuing on to and through college. And so on for their children in turn. The racial differences in adult educational attainment, therefore, result in differences in student achievement. This is partially cultural: more highly educated parents are likely to have more cultural resources in the home and to better understand and more value schooling. And it is partially economic. As we have seen, increasing educational levels are correlated with increased incomes. All other things being equal, higher income families can afford to live in neighborhoods with better schools and can provide more supplementary education opportunities for their students. (Of course, all other things are not equal: higher incomes for Black families often do not bring with them equal opportunities to live in neighborhoods with better schools.)

31

Three-Fifths of an Education

NAEP Mathematics Assessments

Reading is basic to all other education and to nearly all work. On the other hand, mathematics is becoming increasingly important as America and the world transition to a knowledge economy. According to the Program for International Student Assessment (PISA) of the Organization for Economic Co-operation and Development (OECD), for secondary school students, "Mathematical performance measures the mathematical literacy of a 15 year-old

> to formulate, employ and interpret mathematics in a variety of contexts to describe, predict and explain phenomena, recognising the role that mathematics plays in the world . . . A mathematically literate student recognises the role that mathematics plays in the world in order to make well-founded judgments and decisions needed by constructive, engaged and reflective citizens."[9]

PISA ranks American students below the OECD average and below all other countries at a comparable state of economic development for mathematical literacy. One reason for this is America's great racial disparities in mathematics skill and knowledge.

There has been much improvement in African-American mathematics performance over the past quarter century. In 1992 there were virtually no Black students at NAEP grade level in mathematics in fourth grade, while in 2015 nearly one-fifth had reached that level. However, the Black/White racial gap actually widened during that period, from 20 percentage points to 33 percentage points.

NAEP Mathematics: Fourth Grade						
Level	Black		White		B/W Gap	
	1992	2015	1992	2015	1992	2015
Proficient or Above	2%	18%	22%	51%	20	33
Below Basic	78%	35%	32%	10%	46	25

There is a similar situation in eighth grade: in 1992, just 2% of Black students and 24% of White students tested at or above proficient, while in 2015, 13% of Black students and 42% of White students did so. Here, again, the gap increased, from 22 points in 1992 to 29 in 2015, and nearly 90% of Black students were not fully mathematically literate.

NAEP Mathematics: Fourth Grade						
Level	Black		White		B/W Gap	
	1992	2015	1992	2015	1992	2015
Proficient or Above	2%	13%	24%	42%	22	29
Below Basic	81%	53%	34%	19%	47	24

At twelfth grade, extraordinarily small percentages of those Black students remaining in school had mastered mathematics at grade level in either 2005 or 2015. The percentages of White students were also small, but three to five times as great as those of Black students. There was essentially no improvement for any group at twelfth grade between 2005 and 2015 and percentages at or above proficient were markedly lower than eighth grade performance, which was, in turn, lower than that of these of students in grade four. More than two-thirds of Black students are mathematically illiterate (scoring Below Basic) at twelfth grade as are nearly half of White students. Proficiency is double that of National Lunch Program eligible students among both Black and White students from more prosperous families. Nonetheless, half of Black students from relatively prosperous families and a quarter of White students from more prosperous families essentially know no mathematics at twelfth grade.

Why is that? It is suggestive that, according to the National Center for Education Statistics, "for both grades 4 and 8, the percentage of students who had a mathematics teacher with state certification was lower for students eligible for the National School Lunch Program . . . than for non-eligible students and lower for Black students than for White students."[10] Apparently, students do not learn as much from unqualified as from qualified teachers. Hence this country's disastrous international standing in mathematics, resulting from the decisions of school principals, boards of education, superintendents and state officials to distribute access to qualified teachers on the basis of race and income.

Three-Fifths of an Education

NAEP History and Science Assessments

In addition to the basic skills of reading and mathematics, NAEP tests some student subject area knowledge in some grades. U.S. History, for example, is tested in eighth grade. Those history assessments have hardly shown any improvement between the first year for which there is data, 2001, and the most recent year for which there is data, 2014. Very low percentages of Black students eligible for the National Lunch Program and low percentages of eligible White, non-Hispanic, students reach proficiency. There also have been only slight increases in the percentages of students, Black and White, from more prosperous families reaching proficiency, although in this category both groups did better than students from lower-income families and nearly a third of White students from more prosperous families reached proficiency in knowledge of US History.

NAEP has only three years of data for Science, which was also tested at eighth grade. In 2009 very few Black students eligible for the National Lunch Program had reached grade level in Science, and the percentage of Black students ineligible for the program reaching proficiency was only half the percentage of eligible White, non-Hispanic, students. By 2014 there had been a slight improvement for both Black and White eligible groups. Those Black students who were from more prosperous families were approaching the percentage of grade level proficiency of White students eligible for the National Lunch Program. There was some improvement between 2009 and 2015 in the percentage of Black students scoring at the Below Basic of knowledge of Science, less of an improvement was seen among this group of White students. In 2015 nearly half of Black students from more prosperous families scored at the Below Basic level, essentially scientifically illiterate, as did two-thirds of

Three-Fifths of an Education

those eligible for the National Lunch Program. This compares to just 13% of White middle class students and nearly one third of White students eligible for the National Lunch Program.

School Discipline Practices

Among many other factors contributing to educational inequities, there are those of school discipline. The U.S. Department of Education's Office for Civil Rights collects data about school disciplinary actions from all public schools and districts in the United States.[‡‡] "A First Look" of highlights for the 2013-2014 Civil Rights Data Collection was released in October, 2016.[11] Under the heading of "School Discipline," OCR reported: "Black public preschool children are suspended from school at high rates:

> Black preschool children are 3.6 times as likely to receive one or more out-of-school suspensions as white preschool children . . . Black children represent 19% of preschool enrollment, but 47% of preschool children receiving one or more out-of-school suspensions; in comparison, white children represent 41% of preschool enrollment, but [only] 28% of preschool children receiving one or more out-of-school suspensions . . . Black boys represent 19% of male preschool enrollment, but 45% of male preschool children receiving one or more out-of-school suspensions . . . Black girls represent 20% of female preschool enrollment, but 54% of female preschool children receiving one or more out-of-school suspensions.

Professor Walter S. Gilliam of Yale University has found that preschool teachers both expect more disciplinary issues with Black than White children, especially Black boys, and punish Black children, especially Black boys, more severely.[12]

OCR found that "Racial disparities in suspensions are also apparent in K-12 schools:

[‡‡] School discipline data concerns the activities of school personnel in restricting access to education. Suspensions are either in-school or out-of-school and are counted as those inflicted only once during the school year or once or more often. Expulsions can be with or without educational services and those under zero-tolerance policies. There are also data concerning school-related arrests and referrals to law enforcement.

>While 6% of all K-12 students received one or more out-of-school suspensions, the percentage is 18% for black boys; 10% for black girls; 5% for white boys; and 2% for white girls . . . Black K-12 students are 3.8 times as likely to receive one or more out-of-school suspensions as white students . . . Black girls are 8% of enrolled students, but 13% of students receiving one or more out-of-school suspensions. Girls of other races did not disproportionately receive one or more out-of-school suspensions.

Expulsions are the most severe form of school discipline. OCR found that "Black students are expelled from school at disproportionately high rates:

>Black students are 1.9 times as likely to be expelled from school without educational services as white students . . . Black boys represent 8% of all students, but 19% of students expelled without educational services . . . Black girls are 8% of all students, but 9% of students expelled without educational services.

In addition, "Black students are more likely to be disciplined through law enforcement: Black students are 2.2 times as likely to receive a referral to law enforcement or be subject to a school-related arrest as white students . . . [and] Black boys and white boys represent 8% and 26% of all students, respectively, but 18% and 43% of students subject to restraint or seclusion."[13]

Nearly 40% of all Black students and half of male Black students (48%) in grades 6 through 12 have been suspended or expelled at least once, as compared to 16% of White students.[14] Corporal punishment is only used in a few isolated places, such as one or two districts in Louisiana, by White school personnel on Black students, and therefore can be placed in another category, perhaps that of residual Jim Crow traditions encouraging random terrorizing of descendants of enslaved Africans by White residents.

Just as crime statistics measure not crime, but police activity, so rather than simply recording the actions of ill-behaved students, school discipline categories record the actions of school officials: corporal punishment, suspension, expulsions, referral to law enforcement and school-related arrests. All of these actions have the effect of limiting access to educational opportunities, often resulting in the student punished in this way leaving school prematurely.

We can examine the discipline activities of school personnel in rather more detail in, for example, three large urban districts outside the south: Chicago, New York and Philadelphia. Chicago's student enrollment is 46% Hispanic, 40% Black, 10% White, non-Hispanic, and 4% Asian.[§§] In Chicago, only four White, non-Hispanic, students, all male, were expelled—that out of 19,000 male White students. As with the Asian students, the only discipline category in which school personnel saw fit to place White students at a rate equal to their enrollment was that involving a single out-of-school suspension. The number of Hispanic students, also, does not exceed their enrollment representation in any category and in the matter of expulsions varies from 2% to 17% of those expelled under any heading, as compared to the Hispanic enrollment of 46%.

Chicago's school personnel, in contrast, are particularly active in inflicting disciplinary measures on Black students. Sixty-five percent of students receiving one or more in-school suspensions from those schools are Black, as are 60% of those receiving only one out-of-school suspension. Seventy-six percent of those receiving more than one-out of–school suspensions are Black; as are 79% of those expelled with and 88% of those expelled without educational services. Eighty-three percent of those expelled under zero tolerance policies are Black as are 62% of those referred to law enforcement. A number equal to 44% of all male Black students in the Chicago schools was recorded as subjected to one category or another of disciplinary punishment in the 2013 school year. Of course some of those students were double-counted: suspended then expelled and the like. And some would have been disciplined even by the most fair-minded adult. And all are likely to leave school before graduating from high school, likely to be incarcerated, likely to never earn

---

[§§] School personnel anywhere in the country rarely inflict school discipline actions on Asian students. Many of Chicago's discipline categories record no Asian students and in neither Philadelphia nor New York does the percentage of Asian students punished rise to that of the percentage of Asian students in the district.

anything above a poverty wage, likely, perhaps, to murder someone or be murdered themselves.

New York's student enrollment is 41% Hispanic, 26% Black, 15% White and 16% Asian. Only six White students, all male, were expelled—that out of 78,000 male White students. There was no discipline category in which school personnel saw it necessary to place White students at a rate equal to their enrollment. The number of Hispanic students exceeded their enrollment representation in only one sub-category (male students receiving one or more in-school suspensions) and only 14 male Hispanic students were expelled, out of 206,300.

On the other hand, New York's school personnel, like those in Chicago, are particularly active in inflicting disciplinary measures on Black students. Forty-nine percent of students receiving one or more in-school suspensions are Black, as are 54% of those receiving only one out-of-school suspension. Sixty-three percent of those receiving more than one-out of–school suspensions are Black; as are 66% of those expelled with educational services. Forty percent of those expelled under zero tolerance policies are Black as are 53% of those referred to law enforcement. While the school discipline activities of New York City's school personnel are not as frequent as those of their colleagues in Chicago, they are similarly disproportionately inflicted on Black students.

Philadelphia's student enrollment is 19% Hispanic, 53% Black, 15% White and 8% Asian. None of the 21,000 White students were expelled. Sixteen percent of students suspended one or more times were White, as compared with the 15% share of the district enrollment composed of White students. Hardly any Hispanic students were recorded in the discipline matters—eight in all categories other than school-related arrest, where 15% of those in the district were Hispanic, compared to the 19% share of Hispanic students in the district. (It does seem a bit odd that Philadelphia's school personnel take so few actions regarding discipline matters involving Hispanics, other than the very serious items requiring police action, but that is what the district reported to the U.S. Department of Education.)

Philadelphia's school personnel, in contrast, allocate 71% of one or more in-school suspensions to Black students, 84% of only one out-of-school suspensions, and 87% of more than one out-of-school suspensions. Seventy-three percent of students subjected to school-related arrests in Philadelphia are Black. A number equal to nearly a quarter of all male Black students in the Philadelphia schools were subjected to one category or another of disciplinary punishment in the 2013 school year. The school discipline activities of Philadelphia's school personnel are more frequent than those in New York, although not as frequent as those of their colleagues in Chicago. However, they are similarly disproportionately inflicted on Black students. These disproportionalities hold for both male and female students.

Five years ago the Justice Center of the Council of State Governments issued a report entitled "Breaking Schools' Rules: A Statewide Study on How School Discipline Related to Students' Success and Juvenile Justice Involvement." The study established that racial/ethnic disproportionality in school discipline is a function of school personnel actions and attitudes, rather than student behavior. As with Gilliam's research with preschool teachers, it also established that those attitudes, and hence actions, can be changed by in-service professional development. In districts as large as those of Chicago, New York and Philadelphia this might be costly. On the other hand, maintaining the status quo destroys the life-chances, and in many cases the lives, of thousands of Black children.

Three-Fifths of an Education

Graduation Rates and College Preparedness

In the 2013-14 school year, the adjusted cohort graduation rate (ACGR) for public high schools was 82%. But within that total, graduation rates varied dramatically by race: White students graduated at a rate of 87%, Black students graduated at a rate of 73%.[15] However, these rates are exaggerated if we consider that the goal of k-12 education is college- and career-readiness. When the students of the class of 2013-14 were in eighth grade 63% of White students and 89% of Black students did not read at grade level (NAEP proficient or above). If we assume that the 13% of White students and the 27% of Black students who did not graduate were among those not reading at grade level in eighth grade, then by this measure that just 42% of the White students and 14% of the Black students in the cohort graduated prepared for college and careers.

The U.S. Department of Education's Office for Civil Rights (OCR) recently found that "Black and Latino students have less access to high-level math and science courses [than White students]:

33% of high schools with high black and Latino student enrollment[16] offer calculus, compared to 56% of high schools with low black and Latino student enrollment . . . 48% of high schools with high black and Latino student enrollment offer physics, compared to 67% of high schools with low black and Latino student enrollment . . . 65% of high schools with high black and Latino student enrollment offer chemistry, compared to 78% of high schools with low black and Latino student enrollment . . . 71% of high schools with high black and Latino student enrollment offer Algebra II, compared to 84% of high schools with low black and Latino student enrollment.[17]

45

At least partially as a consequence, while 42% of White students are proficient or above in grade eight mathematics, only 12% of Black students reach that level.

OCR found a similar situation in regard to Gifted and Talented (GATE) and Advanced Placement (AP) courses. "Black and Latino students represent 42% of student enrollment in schools offering gifted and talented education (GATE) programs, yet 28% of the students enrolled in GATE programs.

> White students are 49% of all students in schools offering GATE programs and 57% of students in GATE programs . . . Black and Latino students represent 38% of students in schools that offer AP courses, but 29% of students enrolled in at least one AP course.[18]

We might take grade 12 mathematics and science as proxies for AP coursework. When NAEP last measured grade 12 mathematics, in 2015, 30% of White students taking those courses and just 7% of Black students were at grade level. In 2015, 29% of White students and 5% of Black students taking grade 12 science classes were at grade level. Or, in other words, about 95% of Black students were performing below the level approximating AP math and Science. Two-thirds or more were at the Below Basic level: in effect, mathematically and scientifically illiterate.

Not coincidentally, OCR found inequities in the qualifications of teaching staffs. "Black, Latino, and American Indian or Alaska Native students are more likely to attend schools with higher concentrations of inexperienced teachers:

> 7% of black students, 6% of Latino students, and 6% of American Indian or Alaska Native students attend schools where more than 20% of teachers are in their first year of teaching, compared to 3% of white students and 3% of Asian students . . .
>
> 9% of teachers in schools with high black and Latino student enrollment are in their first year of teaching, compared to 5% of teachers in schools with low black and Latino student enrollment.

The SAT is another indicator of college and career preparedness. In 2014-15 schools prepared their students so that the mean scores of college-bound seniors on the SAT Critical Reading test for White students was 529, that for Black students was 431. On the Mathematics test, the mean scores for White students was 534, for Black students 428. The mean Critical Reading score for Black students is at about the 35th percentile of students taking the tests, that for White students at about the 67th. The mean Critical Reading score for Black students corresponds to that for all students with family incomes under $20,000, while that for White students corresponds to all students with family incomes between $100,000 and $120,000.[19] Given family-income-based funding for most public schools, these results are unsurprising, yet another indication of the limited educational opportunities for Black and other low-income students. While 53% of White SAT takers met the SAT College and Career Readiness Benchmark, just 16% of African-American SAT takers met the SAT College and Career Readiness Benchmark. These percentages approximate those in each group testing as proficient in reading when in middle school.[20]

The segregation of American high schools directly affects the chances that minority students will be prepared to go on to college. The U.S. Department of Education has found that as the percentage of students in a high school who are "non-White" increases, the percentage of graduates attending 4-year colleges declines: from 44% for those schools with less than 5% minority to 33% for those with 50% or more.[21] Since "non-White" includes "Asian" as well as Black and Hispanic students, it is highly likely that Black students in those high schools with few non-Black students will have much lower chances of going to college than that. Perhaps as a consequence, only 33% of Black 18- to 24-year olds enroll in colleges, compared to 44% of all 18- to 24-year old White young adults.[22]

Black or African-American students who were full-time, first-time students who were seeking a Bachelor's degree or the equivalent in a 4-year institutions had a graduation rate within six years of 40% in 2016, as compared to 63% for White students. Those attending 2-year institutions had a graduation rate within three years of 25%, compared to 33% for White students.[23] These effects are increasingly evident with each step of further education. While Black

Three-Fifths of an Education

students receive 14% of Associates degrees conferred, they receive only 11% of Bachelor's degrees and just 8% of Doctorates.[24] Just 23% of Black or African-Americans aged 25 years and over have a Bachelor's degrees or higher in 2015, as compared to 36% for White Americans: approximately three-fifths.[25]

What does a High School Diploma Mean?

Much progress has been made in standardizing calculations for high school graduation rates and although there remain local oddities, such as a proliferation of types of high school diplomas, particularly in the South, the overall situation is such as to allow a sharper focus on individual districts. We can, then, begin by looking at three typical large urban districts—Chicago, New York and Philadelphia—with at least a first order degree of confidence that we are looking at similar data among them. (Chicago's graduation rate calculations have been questioned—certain groups are said to be excluded—but that discussion can be put aside for another occasion.)

Those graduation rates are indications of the success, or lack of it, for each of these districts in providing their students with diplomas. How, then, can we assess the degree to which the districts are successful in educating those students, providing them with the skills and knowledge necessary for college and careers? The National Assessment of Educational Progress is of some help in this. The cliché description of NAEP's data is that it is "the gold standard," and there is little doubt that its assessments are accurate. Unfortunately, NAEP does not provide district data for its twelfth grade assessments. We will therefore use the assessments at eighth grade, selecting among the many subject-area assessments that which is most fundamental, reading. We can, with this information, throw some light on the question of how well-educated are those students receiving diplomas from these three cities.

Comparing NAEP 2015 eighth grade reading proficiency and graduation rates for the New York City groups, we find the following:

Three-Fifths of an Education

New York				
	Asian	**Black**	**Hispanic**	**White**
Grade 8 Reading Proficient	41%	15%	22%	46%
Graduation Rate	83%	64%	61%	81%
Ratio (rounded)	2:1	4:1	3:1	2:1

Twice the percentage of Asian and White students, three times the percentage of Hispanic students and more than four times the percentage of Black students graduate from the New York City schools as are reading at grade level in eighth grade.

Comparing NAEP 2015 eighth grade reading proficiency and graduation rates for the Philadelphia groups, we found the following:

Philadelphia				
	Asian	**Black**	**Hispanic**	**White**
Grade 8 Reading Proficient	44%	9%	11%	26%
Graduation Rate	80%	65%	53%	71%
Ratio (rounded)	3:1	7:1	5:1	3:1

Philadelphia is clearly failing to teach reading to most of its students—a remarkable three-quarters of its White students and over 90% of its Black students test below grade level in reading on NAEP's eighth grade evaluation. Nearly three times the percentage of Asian and White students, almost five times the percentage of Hispanic students and nearly seven times the percentage of Black students graduate from the Philadelphia schools as are reading at grade level in eighth grade.

Looking at the results for the Chicago groups, we found the following:

Chicago				
	Asian	**Black**	**Hispanic**	**White**
Grade 8 Reading Proficient	N/A	13%	24%	63%
Graduation Rate	N/A	71%	80%	87%
Ratio (rounded)	N/A	5:1	3:1	1:1

Nearly half again the percentage of White students, more than three times the percentage of Hispanic students and more than five times the percentage of Black students graduate from the Chicago schools as are reading at grade level in eighth grade. And although Chicago's success with White Students is impressive, it fails to teach over 85% of its Black students this fundamental skill. (There are too few Asian students in the Chicago schools for NAEP to report its assessments of their skills.)

On average, then, these three districts graduate about twice the percentage of Asian and White students than are reading at grade level in middle school, while they graduate three-and-a-half times that of Hispanic students and five and-a-half that of Black students.

What happens to these recipients of high school diplomas from the Chicago, New York and Philadelphia schools? Do those diplomas mean that they were educated by their schools so as to be career- and college-ready?

Nationally, according to the most recent data from the National Center for Education Statistics (NCES), 83% of recent Asian high school completers enrolled in a two or four year post-secondary institution, as did 71% of White, 69% of Hispanic and 56% of Black recent high school completers. Given the NAEP data on reading proficiency, there is a reasonable assumption that most graduates from the Chicago, New York and Philadelphia systems, and, in particular, their Black and Hispanic students, initially enroll in community colleges. Again, according to that most recent NCES report, 34% of Asian, 29% of White, 30% of Hispanic and 20% of Black students graduated within 150 percent of normal time in two-year postsecondary institutions. Or, in other words, 80% of Black, 70% of Hispanic and White and 66% of Asian students who attempted an Associates degree were not prepared to succeed. This accords with reports that in New York City, 80% of community college enrollees require remediation.

There is another way of putting this. In Chicago, New York and Philadelphia—and likely in other large cities—the vast majority of Black and Hispanic are either not graduating or are being handed diplomas that mean little. Most of those who receive diplomas graduate without necessary basic skills. Of the half to two-thirds who receive diplomas, another half or two-thirds—a quarter or a third of those who began high school—enroll in college. Of *those,* one-fifth to one-third graduate in the time expected, that is, 5% to 11% of the entering high school classes. These college numbers are from national statistics. It is probably worse than that for Black and Hispanic students in Chicago, New York and Philadelphia, for their peers in Cleveland, Detroit and Memphis.

*   *   *

During the first part of this section we looked at graduation rates and eighth grade reading proficiency for Chicago, New York and Philadelphia. We will now look at five more districts: Cleveland, Detroit and Milwaukee, in the north, and Charlotte, North Carolina, and Duval County (Jacksonville), Florida, in the south. As none of these had statistically significant Asian enrollments, we will consider only Black, Hispanic and White students. Comparing NAEP 2015 eighth grade reading proficiency and graduation rates for the Charlotte groups, we find the following:

Charlotte			
	Black	**Hispanic**	**White**
Grade 8 Reading Proficient	18%	25%	59%
Graduation Rate	87%	80%	94%
Ratio (rounded)	5:1	3:1	2:1

Close to twice the percentage of White students, more than three times the percentage of Hispanic students and nearly five times the percentage of Black students graduate from the Charlotte schools as are reading at grade level in eighth grade.

Comparing NAEP 2015 eighth grade reading proficiency and graduation rates for the Cleveland groups, we find the following:

Cleveland			
	Black	Hispanic	White
Grade 8 Reading Proficient	8%	12%	19%
Graduation Rate	64%	61%	82%
Ratio (rounded)	8:1	5:1	4:1

More than four times the percentage of White students, five times the percentage of Hispanic students and eight times the percentage of Black students graduate from the Cleveland schools as are reading at grade level in eighth grade.

For the Detroit groups, we find the following:

Detroit			
	Black	Hispanic	White
Grade 8 Reading Proficient	5%	16%	N/A
Graduation Rate	77%	81%	N/A
Ratio (rounded)	15:1	5:1	N/A

More than five times the percentage of Hispanic students and more than fifteen times the percentage of Black students graduate from the Detroit schools as are reading at grade level in eighth grade. (There are too few White, non-Hispanic, students in the Detroit schools for NAEP to report its assessments of their skills.)

Comparing NAEP 2015 eighth grade reading proficiency and graduation rates for the Duval County groups, we find the following:

Three-Fifths of an Education

Duval County			
	Black	**Hispanic**	**White**
Grade 8 Reading Proficient	18%	30%	41%
Graduation Rate	71%	74%	81%
Ratio (rounded)	4:1	3:1	2:1

Twice the percentage of White students, two and a half times the percentage of Hispanic students and four times the percentage of Black students graduate from the Duval County schools as are reading at grade level in eighth grade.

And for the Milwaukee groups, we find the following:

Milwaukee			
	Black	**Hispanic**	**White**
Grade 8 Reading Proficient	7%	19%	29%
Graduation Rate	55%	59%	68%
Ratio (rounded)	8:1	3:1	2:1

More than twice the percentage of White students, three times the percentage of Hispanic students and eight times the percentage of Black students graduate from the Milwaukee schools as are reading at grade level in eighth grade.

Only Charlotte taught most of any of these racial/ethnic groups to read proficiently by eighth grade, 59% of its White students. This was three times the level for the district's Black students. And yet Charlotte's results (and those of Duval County) compare well with those of Cleveland, Detroit and Milwaukee, which had results so bad for their Black students that chance effects may have accounted for any success in the districts' efforts for them.

The difference between White, non-Hispanic, graduation rates, on the one hand, and Black and Hispanic rates, on the other, is rather small in these districts, as these things go nationally, varying from about 20 points for Cleveland to about 10 points for the others, except for Detroit, where the difference is inverted—higher Black and Hispanic than White graduation rates. Charlotte's graduation rate for Black students is higher than that for White students in the other districts. Detroit's graduation rate for White students is lower than that for Black students in all the other districts except Milwaukee. All of these districts graduate most of their Black, Hispanic and White students. Charlotte's success in this matter is quite notable.

On average, then, these districts graduate about two and a half times the percentage of White students than are reading at grade level in middle school, while they graduate nearly four times that of Hispanic students and eight times that of Black students. Unless remarkable gains are made in reading proficiency in the schools of these cities between grades 8 and 12, there is only a one in eight chance that their Black high school graduates read at grade level, one in four that their Hispanic graduates do so and less than fifty-fifty that their White diploma recipients can read proficiently. (And given national data, it is unlikely that there are in fact enough gains, if any, between grades 8 and 12 to make a difference.) Of course, those students who are not given diplomas will face bleak futures indeed.

In Charlotte, Cleveland, Detroit, Duval County and Milwaukee, as in Chicago, New York and Philadelphia, the vast majority of Black and Hispanic are either not graduating or are being handed diplomas that mean little. Those diplomas falsely represent preparation for adult life, for further education and training. They are false promises. The federal government has recently taken a firm line with private vocational schools that give out worthless diplomas. It might be appropriate for the U.S. Department of Education to do something similar with districts that give diplomas to their students whom they have qualified for little beyond remedial education.

The first step toward improving this situation is for districts to be honest about their data, in this case, honest when giving out diplomas. The steps that should follow are well-known: providing resources for lower-income and especially Black and Hispanic students at least as generously as they are provided by their schools and families for students from higher income families. If these things are not done, one can only conclude that those who could do them do not wish to do so. Down that path is a society divided between a steadily shrinking, and aging, wealthy America and an increasing, and increasingly impoverished, other America: Black, Brown and, yes, White, non-Hispanics, as well.

Conclusion

It is essential that students—Black, White, poor and not, males and females—learn to read fluently and learn not only particular mathematical operations but to think mathematically. It is no less essential that students learn the fundamentals of science and history, learn to think scientifically and historically, learn how to evaluate evidence and how to conduct research. The U.S. Department of Education finds that at the crucial grade 8 middle school level just fifteen percent of Black students, compared to forty-two percent of White students, read proficiently. By this measure of educational opportunity, perhaps coincidentally, Black students have their historic three-fifths of the opportunities afforded to White students. The U.S. Department of Education also finds that in terms of economic status, just 20% of students from families with incomes of $45,000 or less, read at grade level, while 47% of students from families with incomes higher than that read at grade level. Two-thirds of White families have incomes over that line, while just half of Black families have incomes over $45,000.

Combining these measure, just 12% of Black students from National Lunch Program-eligible families read at grade level, compared to 27% of White students from families with similar low incomes. Black students from families in the upper half of the Black family income distribution read at least at grade level 26% of the time, while twice that proportion of White students with families in the much larger upper two-thirds of the White family income distribution read at grade level. Poverty apparently has a much stronger effect on the educational opportunities of Black students than on those of White students. Increasing family economic status might then be said to have half the favorable effect on educational opportunities for Black as for White students. It is not unlikely that this is an effect of the difference in the quality of schools in Black

57

and White neighborhoods, the former being provided with fewer resources than the latter.

How much of the national education achievement gap is based on family income and parental education and how much derives from the residual category, racial prejudice? We can address this question and then reach some estimates of the size of the equity challenge by using data from three sources: the Census, the U.S. Department of Education's National Assessment of Education Progress, and the U.S. Department of Education's data base of student enrollment by race and grade.

If our goal is to close the racial gap in educational achievement, we might posit as an initial objective closing the racial gap between Black and White students from lower-income families. According to Census data, the National Lunch Program cut-off of eligibility for a family of four, approximately $45,000, makes 48% of Black families eligible. We can, then, make some calculations concerning the *numbers* of Black students currently reading at grade level eligible for the National Lunch Program. There are 583,000 African-American students in eighth grade, indicating that some 280,000 (48%) are eligible for the National Lunch Program. According the NAEP, just 12% of Black students in this category read at grade level. That is 33,600 students. Twenty-seven percent of White lower-income eighth grade students read at grade level, a gap of 15 percentage points. In other words, other things being equal, including income, a White student's school is more than twice as likely as a Black student's school to teach them to read with expected proficiency by middle school. If that gap were closed, an additional 42,000 Black students would read at grade level. Or, we might say that for Black students from lower-income families, the racial penalty is 15%, now paid by those 42,000 students.

A greater goal is to close both the racial and income gaps in educational opportunities. Half of White students from families with incomes over the National Lunch Program cut-off are taught to read at grade level in eighth grade, which is just under twice the 26% of Black students from families with incomes over the National Lunch Program cut-off who are taught to read at grade level in eighth grade. If the gap between Black and White students from higher income families were closed, an additional 72,800 Black students would read at grade level. For Black students from higher income families, the racial penalty, 24%, is even greater than that for Black students from lower-income families. It is likely that this is because given the existing segregation within and between school systems, even Black students from higher income families attend inferior schools and have less of the cultural capital accumulated over generations in many higher income White families.

We can be more ambitious than merely seeking to close the education gaps within income groups. Bringing Black students from lower-income families to the reading proficiency of White students from higher income families would require an increase of 38 percentage points from the current 12% reading at grade level to the 50% level, that is, 106,000 students. We can then add the number of Black students from lower-income families not reading at grade level who would be reading at grade level if they were from higher income White families to the number of Black students from higher income families not reading at grade level who would be reading at grade level if they were from higher income White families. That number is 179,000—30% of those African-American students now in grade 8, who are not now taught to grade level in reading at grade 8 who would be if half of Black students, like half of middle class White students today, achieved that basic skill.

What would be the long-term effects of 291,500 African-American students, rather than less than half that—112,500—being as well-prepared by their middle schools as middle class White students? More than twice as many would graduate college- and career-ready. One measure of such preparedness is the college graduation rate. In 2013, the most recent date for which this information is available, twice the percentage of White students (43%) than Black students (21%) graduated from college in four years. (This 22-point gap held as well for those graduating in six years (63% v. 41%).[26]) That year, 191,180 Black undergraduates received Bachelor's degrees. Half of those had achieved that distinction in four years, close to a third in five years, the rest in six or more. For the sake of illustration, we might take it that the typical cohort was approximately 95,000. That is not far off the number of

Three-Fifths of an Education

Black eighth graders who are currently brought to grade level in reading. Given that the percentage of White undergraduates receiving a Bachelor's degree in four years is twice that of Black students, and the percentage of White eighth graders from higher income families reading at grade level is twice that of their Black peers, it seems possible that closing the racial and income gaps in middle school will also go far toward closing that in college graduation rates. And higher college graduation rates would lead to higher incomes (and lower incarceration rates), longer lives and the possibility of increased socio-economic mobility for the next generation.

If this were to come about, the lives of the descendants of enslaved Africans would, finally, no longer be counted as only three-fifths as significant as those of other Americans.

Notes

[1] Department of Defense. 2014 Demographics: Profile of the Military Community.
http://www.militaryonesource.mil/footer?content_id=279104

[2] Median earnings for full-time, year-round workers (male).

[3] Military family incomes were estimated as not substantially different from incomes of similar civilian families by MacDermid, Shelley M., et al. The Financial Landscape for Military Families of Young Children. Technical Report. Military Family Research Institute, Purdue University.
https://www.mfri.purdue.edu/resources/public/reports/Financial%20Landscape%20of%20Families.pdf

[4] Median earnings for full-time, year-round workers (male).

[5] Military family incomes were estimated as not substantially different from incomes of similar civilian families by MacDermid, Shelley M., et al. The Financial Landscape for Military Families of Young Children. Technical Report. Military Family Research Institute, Purdue University.
https://www.mfri.purdue.edu/resources/public/reports/Financial%20Landscape%20of%20Families.pdf

[6] Results for Asian and Hispanic students are not considered separately in order to retain a focus on educational issues affecting Black students.

[7] The results reported for twelfth grade, in 1992, were that 16% of the remaining Black students and 44% of White students read at or above proficient, while in 2015 the results were exactly the same. The percentages at Below Basic were 41% and 16%, respectively, in 1992 and 49% and 22% in 2015. Therefore, we might say, with all due cautions, that at twelfth grade there was effectively no improvement between 1992 and 2015 for either group at the high end, and some worsening at the low end of the reading ability scale.

[8] United States Census. Table DP03. Selected Economic Characteristics: 2005-2009 . 2005-2009 American Community Survey 5-Year Estimates.

[9] https://data.oecd.org/pisa/mathematics-performance-pisa.htm

[10] Rahman, T., Fox, M.A., Ikoma, S., and Gray, L. (2017). Certification Status and Experience of U.S. Public School Teachers: Variations Across Student Subgroups (NCES 2017-056). U.S. Department of Education, National Center for Education Statistics. Washington, DC: U.S. Government Printing Office. nces.ed.gov/pubs2017/2017056.pdf

[11] U.S. Department of Education, Office for Civil Rights. 2013-2014 Civil Rights Data Collection: A First Look, Key Data Highlights on Equity and

Opportunity Gaps in Our Nation's Public Schools, October, 2016, p. 3.
https://www2.ed.gov/about/offices/list/ocr/docs/2013-14-first-look.pdf
[12] See, for example, Gilliam, Walter S. PhD, et al., Do Early Educators'
Implicit Biases Regarding Sex and Race Relate to Behavior Expectations
and Recommendations of Preschool Expulsions and Suspensions? Yale
University Child Study Center // September 28, 2016.
http://ziglercenter.yale.edu/publications/Preschool%20Implicit%20Bias%20
Policy%20Brief_final_9_26_276766_5379.pdf.
[13] U.S. Department of Education, Office for Civil Rights. 2013-2014 Civil
Rights Data Collection: A First Look, Key Data Highlights on Equity and
Opportunity Gaps in Our Nation's Public Schools, October, 2016, pp. 4-5.
https://www2.ed.gov/about/offices/list/ocr/docs/2013-14-first-look.pdf
[14] https://nces.ed.gov/programs/digest/d15/tables/dt15_233.20.asp
[15] National Center for Education Statistics. The Condition of Education.
May, 2016. https://nces.ed.gov/programs/coe/indicator_coi.asp
[16] "'High/low black and Latino enrollment' refers to schools with more than
75 percent and less than 25 percent black and Latino student enrollment,
respectively."
[17] U.S. Department of Education, Office for Civil Rights. 2013-2014 Civil
Rights Data Collection: A First Look, Key Data Highlights on Equity and
Opportunity Gaps in Our Nation's Public Schools, October, 2016, p. 6.
https://www2.ed.gov/about/offices/list/ocr/docs/2013-14-first-look.pdf
[18] U.S. Department of Education, Office for Civil Rights. 2013-2014 Civil
Rights Data Collection: A First Look, Key Data Highlights on Equity and
Opportunity Gaps in Our Nation's Public Schools, October, 2016, p. 7.
https://www2.ed.gov/about/offices/list/ocr/docs/2013-14-first-look.pdf
[19] College Board. SAT. 2015 College-Bound Seniors. Total Group Profile
Report. https://secure-media.collegeboard.org/digitalServices/pdf/sat/total-
group-2015.pdf
[20] https://secure-media.collegeboard.org/digitalServices/pdf/2015-college-
board-results-national-report.pdf
[21] https://nces.ed.gov/programs/digest/d15/tables/dt15_302.40.asp
[22] https://nces.ed.gov/programs/digest/d15/tables/dt15_302.20.asp;
https://nces.ed.gov/programs/digest/d15/tables/dt15_302.65.asp
[23] Ginder, S.A., Kelly-Reid, J.E., and Mann, F.B. (2016). Graduation Rates
for Selected Cohorts, 2007–12; Student Financial Aid,
Academic Year 2014–15; Admissions in Postsecondary Institutions, Fall
2015: First Look (Provisional Data) (NCES 2017-084). U.S.

Department of Education. Washington, DC: National Center for Education Statistics. Retrieved [date] from http://nces.ed.gov/pubsearch.

[24] https://nces.ed.gov/programs/digest/d15/tables/dt15_324.20.asp; https://nces.ed.gov/programs/digest/d15/tables/dt15_324.20.asp

[25] https://nces.ed.gov/programs/digest/d15/tables/dt15_104.10.asp? current=yes

[26] Musu-Gillette, L., Robinson, J., McFarland, J., KewalRamani, A., Zhang, A., and Wilkinson-Flicker, S. (2016). Status and Trends in the Education of Racial and Ethnic Groups 2016 (NCES 2016-007). U.S. Department of Education, National Center for Education Statistics. Washington, DC. Retrieved May 16, 2017 from http://nces.ed.gov/pubsearch.

Black Students In The Former Confederate States

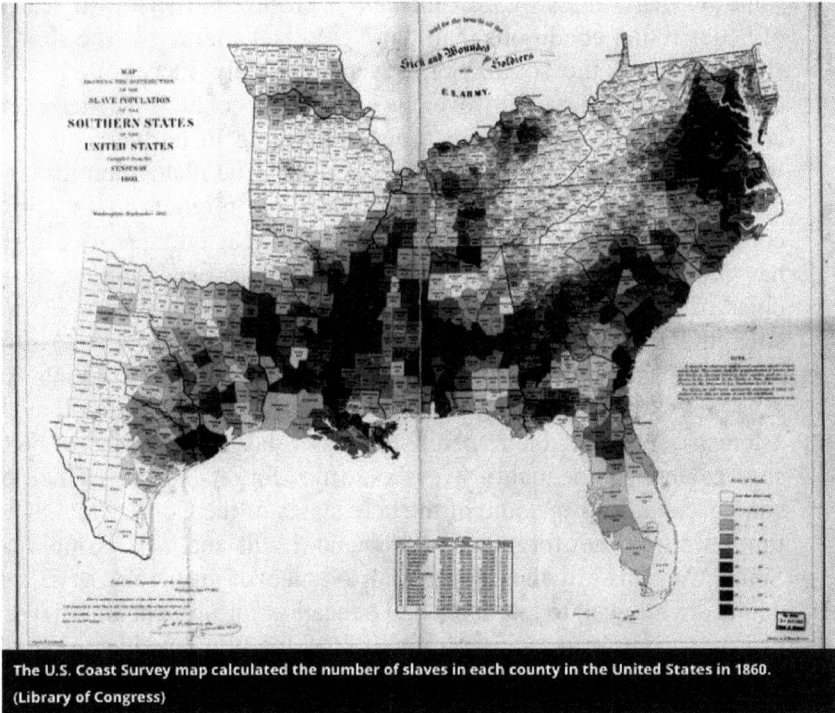

The U.S. Coast Survey map calculated the number of slaves in each county in the United States in 1860.
(Library of Congress)

The schools of the U.S. Department of Defense demonstrate what African-American students can achieve in schools that simply do not ration educational opportunities and resources by race. Unfortunately, this is a virtually unique situation in this country. Most people know that the descendants of enslaved Africans living in the United States have, on average, lower-incomes and less education than their White fellow citizens. Perhaps it is taken for granted—by those White fellow citizens. However, we should not accept this as natural. It is not natural. It is a condition created by specific people, acting individually and in groups: governors, state legislators, chief state school officers, members of state and local boards of education, school district superintendents, mayors and members of city and county legislatures.

The Great Migration of the early twentieth century colonized some northern cities by descendants of enslaved Africans in search of better living conditions than those they had endured in the former slave states of the south. Some were relatively successful in this endeavor, for a time. However, over the past couple of generations conditions for many African-Americans living in northern cities— from Buffalo to Cleveland—have worsened. The realization that the promise of equality that was the "pull" of the migration (Jim Crow constituting the "push"), the realization that that promise was false, has focused attention on the failure of public education in those cities, the rise of mass incarceration, and the maintenance, if not strengthening, of segregation.

While contemplating the hypocrisy of responsible officials in, say, New York City, with their increasingly tiresome expressions of astonishment that their neighborhoods and schools have been segregated into inequality, we should not forget the persistence of similar conditions in some of the core states of the Confederacy. Old times are truly not forgotten in Alabama, Louisiana, Mississippi and South Carolina. In those states an average of just 15% of Black adults are allowed to attain enough education for a Bachelor's degree or better, compared to an average of 26% for White residents. South Carolina is the champion in this matter, the state with the largest gap, providing educations resulting in Bachelor's degrees for nearly a third, 31%, of its White adults, but for less than half that percentage, 15%, for its Black residents. At the other end of the educational attainment scale, the region leaves an average of 22% of its Black adults without any education qualifications whatsoever, but only 14% of its White adults are without high school diplomas.

The national averages for all racial and ethnic groups for these measures are 30% for college graduates, 14% for those without high school diplomas.

In other words, these states educate White residents to U.S. national averages, leaving their Black residents in an educational condition not found elsewhere among the developed countries of the world.

Just like old times.

As a consequence, or, perhaps, as just another part of the same effort at maintaining the *status quo pro ante*, the average Black family income in the former slave states is just over $34,000, that of White families nearly $64,000. Here the champion is Louisiana, with a $35,000 spread, the $68,000 White family income more than double that of Black families in the state. Hence the contrast, for example, between the Ninth Ward of New Orleans and that city's Garden District. The average poverty rate of White people in these states, 13%, is actually lower than the national average (16%), and, of course, less than half that of their Black "fellow citizens," which is 32%. Here again, we look to South Carolina for the extremes of inequity. The poverty rate of South Carolina's under-educated Black residents is three times that of their White neighbors.

Aside from the "racial penalty" at each income level of approximately 20% for those adults who have finished high school, income is largely determined by education, at least among people who work for a living, rather than inheriting, say, real estate fortunes. Given the racial disparities in educational attainment in these states, the racial disparities in income follow directly. But how do these racial disparities in educational attainment come about?

An effective way for those officials responsible for schools and school systems to accomplish this is to limit reading ability. If a person is unable to read at, say, the level expected of middle school students in eighth grade, they are unlikely to learn much in their remaining school years, unlikely to earn a meaningful high school diploma, unlikely to attend and graduate from college or to earn an income above the poverty level.

Officials in Alabama, Louisiana, Mississippi and South Carolina do well at this task. The usual measure used for such comparisons is the National Assessment of Educational Progress grade 8 test results. In Alabama, Louisiana, Mississippi and South Carolina, about two-thirds of Black students, but only one-third of White students have family incomes low enough to make them eligible for the National Lunch Program. That is something to keep in mind as we look at reading achievement scores in the former slave states.

67

Three-Fifths of an Education

We can begin by noting that the overall percentage of Black students in these states who read well enough in eighth grade to be assessed by NAEP as "proficient or above" is 11%. That is, nearly 90% read eighth grade material either with difficulty or really not at all. On the other hand, thirty-four percent of White, non-Hispanic, students in Alabama, Louisiana, Mississippi and South Carolina are assessed as proficient or above when they are tested on eighth grade reading. (The national percentage for all students in public schools is 33%.) The schools in these states manage to teach only one-third the percentage of their Black students to read at grade level as the national average for all students or as they do for their White students. The champion here is Mississippi, which teaches necessary reading skills to four times the percentage of its White students as to its Black students.

We can look a little more deeply into this. Nationally, one-third of White, non-Hispanic, family incomes are below $45,000 per year, making their children eligible for the National Lunch Program. Twice that percentage, two-thirds of Black families have incomes below $45,000 per year. Among the Black students in the states on which we are focusing here, whose family incomes are below the National Lunch Program cut-off, on average, just 9% are taught to read fluently, as compared to 25% of the White students from families with those low incomes. Proficiency scores for White students from relatively impoverished families in Alabama, Louisiana, Mississippi and South Carolina are in a tight range: 24% to 26%. Despite that, Mississippi's officials responsible for these inequities are again the clear winners, with an 18% point spread between the 7% of its low-income Black students and 25% of its low-income White students reading at grade level in middle school.

Among the one-third of Black students from more prosperous families in these states, 22% are taught to read to the level expected of eighth graders, compared to 41% of the two-thirds of White students from those relatively prosperous families. Here, it is South Carolina's officials responsible for education who are the definite winners in the education inequality competition with a 23% point spread, anchored by a remarkable 46% record with its White students from comparatively prosperous families. Perhaps these racial

68

differences among students from families with similar incomes have something to do with differing qualities of education on offer for students of each race.

The final step in the public schools toward achieving educational attainment levels typical of those in developed countries is high school graduation. For the nation as a whole, the reported graduation rate for Black students is 75%, that for White, non-Hispanic, students 88%. Alabama, Louisiana, Mississippi and South Carolina report that an average of 78% of their Black students graduate, as do 86% of their White students. This is remarkable, considering that only 11% of their Black students and 34% of their White students could read at grade level in middle school and just 15% of the former and 26% of the latter turn out to be well enough prepared to continue on to a college degree.

The regional outlier in these matters is Georgia. That state, with a similar history to that of the other Black Belt states of slavery, Civil War devastation, Jim Crow and "massive resistance" to school integration, nonetheless exhibits socio-economic and education indicators remarkably close to national averages. Educational attainment for Black adults in Georgia (23% bachelor's degree or above) is slightly higher than the national average for Black adults of 20%. Median income for Georgia's Black families is about the same as the national average for Black families and the state's Black poverty rate is lower. Sixteen percent of Georgia's Black students in eighth grade are brought to grade level in reading, compared to the national average of 15% for Black students, and the percentage of Black students eligible for the National Lunch Program reading at grade level (12%) is identical to the national average for eligible Black students. The percentage of African-American students ineligible for the National Lunch Program, those from middle class families, reaching proficiency, 31%, is quite a bit higher than the 26% national average for this group.

It is probably not great praise to observe that Georgia does not do worse than most states in the Union despite its heritage of slavery and Jim Crow, but Georgia's record is certainly notable in contrast to the disgraceful records of its neighbors. It shows what can be done, even in the south, and the challenges that remain. Apparently, in this case, that which has been done is to work at both ends of the education ladder. Since 1995 Georgia has funded universal pre-school, the benefits of which are well-known. In 2014-15, 59% of the state's 4-year-olds were enrolled in the state's prekindergarten program. (The national average is 29% of 4-year-olds and 5% of 3-year-olds.*) Georgia also has a fully-articulated (credits transfer smoothly among its colleges) and essentially tuition-free system of post-secondary education for low-income students. The state's remaining challenge is the still widely differing results by race of its k-12 system. In education it is not sufficient to be no worse than a national average that is itself an international disgrace.

If education for the descendants of enslaved Africans is to be improved, responsibility and action must be focused on, and taken at, the state and local level. We will, then, next look at the core states of the Confederacy and then look at some other states with large populations of descendants of enslaved Africans.

Three-Fifths of an Education

Selected State Data

As it is possible that some readers may wish to concentrate on particular states, rather than reviewing all those presented in this section, there is a certain amount of unavoidable repetition in formats and definitions, for which I apologize to those who, instead, persist through the entire group.

For historical reasons, education in the United States is a more or less local responsibility, primarily that of school districts, but in part that of states, rather minimally that of the federal government. The Supreme Court can rule from on high that among the results of segregation are inherently unequal educational opportunities, but it does not take George Wallace to ensure that the writ of the court stops at the schoolhouse door. The decisions that result in restricted educational opportunities for the descendants of enslaved Africans are made by school and district administrators, members of local school boards, in some cases by mayors. They are made by the chiefs and staffs of state departments of education and, yes, by governors and state legislatures.

In some states the descendants of enslaved Africans comprise a quarter or more of the population. In other states there are few African-Americans, either as a percentage of the population or in absolute numbers. Our focus will be on the core states of the Confederacy and Maryland, in which slavery was legal until the end of the Civil War. We will add to these a second group, the other states that have a million or more Black or African-American residents. An analysis of data from states in both these groups will provide a more detailed picture of the state-level operations of Jim Crow education today.

NAEP eighth grade reading will be our basic indicator of educational achievement. Reading is the essential skill, NAEP assessments are agreed to be valid, and eighth grade is a crucial point in the education of students. It is the point at which some students have been taught what they need to know and be able to do for

73

success in life, while for others it is the point where they begin to give up on school or where school officials give up on them.

This table shows the African-American populations and percentages of the former slave states, sorted by percentage:

State	Black or African-American Population	Percentage Black or African-American
Mississippi	1,074,200	37%
Louisiana	1,506,534	32%
Georgia	3,150,435	31%
Maryland	1,798,593	30%
South Carolina	1,290,684	28%
Alabama	1,251,311	26%
North Carolina	2,048,628	22%
Delaware	191,814	21%
Virginia	1,551,399	20%
Tennessee	1,055,689	17%
Florida	2,999,862	16%
Texas	2,979,598	12%
Total (Average)	20,898,747	(24%)

The next table shows the African-American populations and percentages of the other states with more than one million African-American residents.

Jurisdiction	Black or African-American Population	Percentage Black or African-American
New York	3,073,800	15%
Illinois	1,866,414	15%
New Jersey	1,204,826	14%
Michigan	1,400,362	14%
Ohio	1,407,681	12%
Pennsylvania	1,377,689	11%
California	2,299,072	7%
Total (Average)	12,629,844	(13%)

We will start with a comparison between Mississippi and Michigan, a southern and northern state that seem quite different, but from the point of view of the education of African-American students are, unfortunately, rather similar.

Three-Fifths of an Education

Mississippi and Michigan

Mississippi and Michigan, one a former slave state, the other a destination of the Great Migration, are the states with the lowest percentage of African-American students reading at or above grade level in eighth grade. Mississippi teaches just 8% of its Black students to read to national standards in middle school; Michigan teaches just 9%. (The national average for Black students is 15%, that of the Department of Defense schools 38%.) And in both states, about half of African-American eighth grade students are functionally illiterate, testing at the Below Basic level by the National Assessment of Educational Progress. As the percentage of students reading at grade level changes little or not at all between eighth and twelfth grade, this means that over 90% of Black students in these states are unlikely to graduate from high school college- and career-ready.

It would, of course, appear to be unjust to say that in the 21st century the goal of educators in Michigan and Mississippi is to so limit educational opportunities for Black students that 90% cannot read at grade level in middle school, that half are functionally illiterate, that nearly a fifth of Black adults in Michigan and a quarter of those in Mississippi have not finished high school. But what else can we say about institutions, and those in responsible positions in those institutions, that year after year fail to meet their responsibilities ninety percent of the time?

Mississippi, the quintessential post-Confederate state, has at 37% the nation's highest percentage of descendants of enslaved Africans. In Michigan, far to the north, only 14% of the population is Black, although there are many more African-Americans in Michigan, 1.4 million, than in Mississippi—1.1 million. Mississippi did not repeal its constitutionally mandated restrictions on voting by means of poll taxes and literacy tests until 1975, nor the requirement for segregated schools until 1978 (a quarter century after *Brown*). Michigan has never had a poll tax or a literacy test for the franchise, nor (unlike some other northern states) *de jure* segregated schools. While the Black population of Mississippi is fairly evenly distributed about the state, although especially dense in the plantation counties along the Mississippi river, that of Michigan is concentrated in its southeastern corner, primarily the formerly highly industrialized cities of Detroit, Flint and Saginaw. The Brown University segregation index for the Detroit metropolitan area is 80, on a scale where 60 is considered very high. A Black student in the Detroit schools is rarely in a class with a White student, rarely in a class with a student who is not from a lower-income family.

Despite their similarities, there are major differences in the ways that the two states distribute, or, rather, restrict, educational opportunities. In Michigan, over half of Black families and one-third of White families have incomes low enough to qualify their children for free- or reduced-price school lunches; in Mississippi, over one-third of White families and over two-thirds of Black families have qualifying incomes (or qualifying lack of incomes). Both states educate very few of their children, of either race, from low-income families. Each brings just 7% of their African-American children from low-income families to reading proficiency in eighth grade. Mississippi manages this marginally better than Michigan for its White students from comparatively poor families: 25% to 23%. The picture is quite different among students from more prosperous families. Mississippi does much better than Michigan for those among them who are descendants of enslaved African, educating just over a quarter to reading proficiency in eighth grade, which we should note is more than either state does for its impoverished White students. Michigan only manages to bring 12% of its students from the upper half of the Black family income distribution to grade level in reading in middle school. Nearly four times that percentage of middle class White children in Michigan learn to read proficiently in eighth grade.

One interpretation of these results would be that while educational opportunity in Mississippi's public schools is chiefly distributed by income for both Black and White students, in Michigan, educational opportunities are chiefly distributed by race, with less regard to income. The gap between lower-income Black and White students in each state is approximately the same, but that between higher income Black and White students is much larger in Michigan. More than twice the percentage of Black students from higher income families in Mississippi are brought to grade level in reading than in Michigan. However, it should be noted that while among White residents of Mississippi, almost two-thirds have incomes high enough to make students from those families *ineligible* for the National Lunch Program, among Black residents, just over one-third have incomes sufficient to make their students ineligible for the National Lunch Program. In other words, dividing educational resources by economic class in Mississippi results in increased opportunities for two-thirds of those from White families and decreased opportunities for two-thirds of those from Black families.

At the classroom level, out-of-school suspensions in both states are inflicted on a racial basis. Schools in Mississippi give Black students more than one-out-of-school suspension three times as often as they do to White students; Michigan does this four times as often to Black as White students, resulting in nearly a fifth of Michigan's Black students being kept out of the classroom at some point in there school careers. Research has shown that out-of-school suspensions have an efficient negative effect on student learning and frequently lead to the need to repeat grades and, eventually, to leaving school without a diploma. Other research has shown that racial disparities in discipline data are an artifact of the differences in racial attitudes among school level administrators and teachers, rather than differences in student behavior.

Mississippi reports a graduation rate for its Black students of 77%, for its White students, 83%, a six-percentage point racial difference, considerably less than the 13% national difference. Michigan reports a graduation rate for its Black students of 68%, for its White students, 83%, close to a 15% racial difference. This is bad enough. But if we look at the basic skill of reading mastered by these

79

students when they were in eighth grade, we can conclude that just 10% of Black students in Michigan and Mississippi graduate able to read at least at the level desired for middle school students.

The failure of Michigan to adequately educate its Black residents can be traced to the inequitable support of the schools they attend. Support for public education in Michigan is directly related to the racial make-up of the schools in each district. In the schools of Ann Arbor—where the University of Michigan is located—the schools are more than 90% White. The median family income is considerably higher than the state average, as are teacher salaries. The pupil-to-teacher ratio is lower (better) than the state average.

Nearly 200,000 of Michigan's 280,000 Black public school students are in the districts of the Detroit metropolitan area and nearby Flint. In Detroit, with a student enrollment that is 80% Black and a median family income just above half of the state average, teachers are paid less than the state average and the pupil-to-teacher ratio is considerably higher. In Detroit, with a majority African-American population of 538,000,[1] relatively few Black adults have advanced educations, a percentage far above the national average are without high school diplomas. Detroit's African-American median family income is very low and far below national average for the group. The Black unemployment and poverty rates in Detroit are extremely high.

Black					
	BA and Higher	No HS Diploma	Family Income	Unemployed	Poverty Rate
Detroit	11%	21%	$33,900	26%	29%
U.S.	20%	15%	$45,000	11%	25%

Nearly 60% of Black students in Detroit's public schools were at the Below Basic level in 2015, that is, functionally illiterate. (There were too few White students in the Detroit public schools to meet NAEP reporting standards.) Among Black students in the Detroit public schools, just 5% read at or above the proficient level (as do just 4% of those eligible for the National Lunch Program).

The 4-year adjusted cohort graduation rate reported by Detroit for the 2014-15 school year was 77% for Black students.[2] Given that only 7% of Black students were reading at grade level in 2011, when they were in eighth grade, it appears that 68-70% of graduating Black students in Detroit received their diplomas while having serious deficiencies in their reading skills. If Black graduation rates and percentages proficient at graduation were equal to current White outcomes, each year there would be an additional 7,700 college and career ready Black high school graduates in Michigan (up from 1,200) and an additional 4,400 in Mississippi (up from 1,100).

The Detroit public schools are under state control and therefore the state government—the legislature and the governor—are directly responsible for how they educate, or fail to educate, their students. The decisions leading to these disparities are not "institutional" or "structural." They are the decisions of the governor and the legislature of the state of Michigan to give few educational opportunities to the descendants of enslaved Africans, children for whose education they are individually and collectively responsible.

Most school districts in Mississippi are rural. Just 7% of Black students in those districts read at grade level in middle school. The only urban districts in Mississippi with large numbers of Black students are the public schools in the state capitol, Jackson, enrolling 28,000 Black students and those in Desoto County, in the far northwest corner of the state, near Memphis, which enroll 11,000. NAEP has not found any students in these or other urban schools in Mississippi reading at grade level or above in eighth grade. According to a lawsuit recently filed by the Southern Poverty Law Center: "Thirteen of the state's 19 school districts that receive an "F" rating [from the state] are more than 95 percent African-American.

The remaining six range from 81 percent to 91 percent African-American. The state's top five highest-performing school districts are predominantly white. The differences reflect the disparities found in schools across the state based on whether a school's enrollment is predominantly African-American or predominantly white.[3]

Private schools have little effect on the educational opportunities of Black students from low-income families in either Mississippi and Michigan. This may be because private school tuition in Mississippi for a family with two children, one in elementary school and one in high school, would amount to nearly a third of the family income of the average Black family in the state. Similarly, an average Black family in Michigan, with two children, one in elementary school and one in high school, would have to find nearly 40% of its income to pay for their private school tuition. No Black students in Mississippi and only 6% of students in Michigan attending charter schools read at or above grade level in eighth grade.

Michigan and Mississippi have taken different paths to limiting educational opportunities for the descendants of enslaved Africans. That followed by Michigan is the racially targeted unequal distribution of educational resources. That followed by Mississippi is economically focused disparities in education quality in the context of centuries of Black poverty. They both work equally well to perpetuate the status of descendants of enslaved Africans as three-fifths of an American.

College graduation is increasingly important for employment and other economic and social matters. In Michigan, college graduation rates for both Black and White adults are lower than national averages: 29% of White residents have a Bachelor's degree or higher and 17% of Black residents, compared to the national averages of 32% and 20%, respectively. The college graduation rate for Black residents of Michigan is almost exactly three-fifths of the White college graduation rate in the state. In large part because of the state's failure to educate its African-American students, while the median family income of White residents is $68,300, that of Black residents is only just over half of that: $37,100. The poverty rate for Black families in Michigan is three and a half times that for White families.

In Mississippi, the state's percentage of Black adults with Bachelor's degrees (14%) is also three-fifths of the percentage of White adults with Bachelor's degrees or higher (24%). The unemployment rate for African-Americans in the state is more than twice that for White residents. The median family incomes of both White and Black Mississippi residents are also considerably below national averages. That of White residents is $62,200, that of Black residents is, again, just over half that: $32,500, hardly different from the ratio in Michigan. The poverty rate for Mississippi's Black families is three times that for White families.

Recently, the director of the Michigan Department of Health and Human Services was charged with misconduct in office, a felony, for his role in the Flint water crisis. It is an interesting precedent. The officials—governors, legislators, members of state and local boards of education and others—who have been responsible for restricting educational opportunities for Black residents of these states could act differently. They could provide the resources needed to close the gaps between the education now provided to their Black students and that provided to their White students. They could improve educational opportunities for all students. They have not. They do not. It is not because they cannot; it is because they will not.

Three-Fifths of an Education

Alabama and Georgia

Unlike Michigan and Mississippi, Alabama and Georgia are neighboring states with similar histories. Both were slave states, core members of the Confederacy, centers of resistance to desegregation. Alabama has the nation's sixth highest percentage of African-American residents, 26% (1.3 million).[4] Georgia has a percentage of African-American residents just over the national average, but one of the larger Black populations in terms of absolute numbers (3.2 million). The Black population of these states was historically concentrated in an east-west band running across the southern third of each state, part of the "Black Belt." According to researcher Raj Chetty and his colleagues, children's chances of reaching the top 20% of income distribution, given parental income in the bottom 20%, is less than 5% in these counties.[5] In other words, poor families in rural Alabama and Georgia are highly likely to remain poor, generation after generation. But although more than a quarter of Alabama's Black population remains rural, only 16% of Georgia's Black population lives in its rural areas. Georgia is dominated by the Atlanta metropolitan area with more than half of the state's total population and more than half the state's Black population. On the other hand, the metropolitan area of Birmingham, Alabama's largest city, contains less than a quarter of the state's population and also less than a quarter of the state's Black population.

The two states differ greatly in terms of educational attainment. More of Alabama's Black adults have not finished high school than have a college education, while that situation is reversed in Georgia, where the percentage of college-educated African-American adults is similar to that of college-educated White adults in Alabama. Likewise, the percentage of Black adults without high school diplomas in Georgia is the same as that for White adults in Alabama.

Three-Fifths of an Education

However, although median Black family incomes in Georgia are higher than those in Alabama, and the poverty rate lower, the racial differences in these categories are similar in the two states: in both states Black unemployment is twice that of White unemployment, Black poverty rates more than twice those for White residents. Taking these indicators together, Georgia's population looks like the United States in most respects (although slightly better educated), Alabama does not. By most measures, those for Black residents of Georgia slightly exceed the "three-fifths" determined for the descendants of enslaved Africans by the Founders, while those of Alabama do not even make it to that level.

Educational Achievement

Georgia schools, in general, educate their students to approximately the national averages, inequities and all, which therefore means educating nearly three times as many of their White students as their Black students to read at grade level in the crucial eighth grade year. Such differences in racial education levels, even in an otherwise exceptional southern state like Georgia, are all too often taken for granted. They should not be. They should not be accepted.

The situation in Alabama is worse. Alabama schools, in general, do not educate their students to the national averages for either race. Within that deficient context, they educate only a little over a third as many of their Black students as their White students to read at grade level in the crucial eighth grade school year. Not only do nearly 90% of Black students and nearly 70% of White students in Alabama's eighth grade classrooms read less well than expected, twenty percent of White students and nearly half, 45%, of Black students test at the Below Basic level in reading in grade eight. They are functionally illiterate. These students have little chance of succeeding in school, graduating with a meaningful diploma, achieving positive socio-economic mobility for themselves or their children.

Student educational attainment in both Alabama and Georgia is further sharply divided by income differences within races. Only a quarter of students from the 36% of White families living in or near poverty in Alabama, and therefore eligible for the National Lunch Program, read at grade level in eighth grade, while more than one-third of other White students, those from more prosperous families, are taught how to read at grade level in eighth grade. Among Black students, just 10% of those from the 62% of Black families eligible for the National Lunch Program in Alabama are taught to read at or above the proficient level, while nearly twice that proportion, 17%, of those from the more prosperous third of Black families have been taught to do so. But this is still much lower than the national average of 26% of National Lunch Program ineligible Black students.

On the other hand, both Black and White families in Georgia are unusually likely to have incomes above the cut-off for National Lunch Program eligibility and within that middle class group the racial divide for educational achievement is not as distinct as in many other states. A Black student from a comparatively prosperous family in Georgia is as likely to be brought to grade level in eighth grade reading as a National Lunch Program eligible (that is, poorer) White student either in Georgia or nationally. Nonetheless, a White student from a comparatively prosperous family in Georgia is four times as likely to be brought to grade level in eighth grade reading than a Black student from a low-income family in that state. The relatively high achievement rate for middle class Black students in Georgia is traceable to Atlanta, where 48% of this group are at or above grade level in eighth grade, about the same as the statewide figure for economically similar White students. Since, again unusually, nearly half of the state's Black families have incomes sufficient to be ineligible for the National Lunch Program, this is an even more important outcome than it would be in the neighboring states with their lesser proportions of higher income Black families.

While income is a highly influential factor in the education of both races in Georgia, educational opportunities are all about race in Alabama. Alabama's schools fail to educate Black students to national averages, regardless of family income classification. Alabama's students from the lowest income White families are much more often educated so as to be able to read proficiently than students from the highest income Black families in the state, unlike in Georgia, where racism is tempered by the influence of economic class.

87

Three-Fifths of an Education

There are great differences in reading achievement between urban and rural schools for White students in both states. Close to half of White students in Alabama's cities reach grade level in reading in eighth grade, but only just over a quarter of those in the state's rural schools do so. More than half of White students in Georgia's cities and suburbs reach grade level in reading in eighth grade, but only 35% of those in the state's rural schools do so. School location also matters for Black students in Georgia, 15% of whom in city schools and 19% in suburban schools read at grade level in eighth grade, but only 10% of Black students in Georgia's rural schools do so. With Alabama's Black students location hardly matters at all: roughly 90% in city schools and rural schools and 85% in suburban schools are not taught to read at grade level in eighth grade, as is the case for 90% of Black students in rural schools. That 90% below proficiency reading level for Black students in Alabama's and Georgia's rural schools is a heritage of slavery in the Black Belt and the failure of today's officials of each state to properly support majority Black rural schools.

Some Other Influences: prekindergarten

Research has shown that effective pre-school programs result in better educational achievement for participating students at least through grade 4. Alabama does not have universal prekindergarten. It does have a prekindergarten program, on paper; it simply does not adequately fund it. As a consequence, just 7,200 students, 12% of the state's 4-year olds, are enrolled in the state's prekindergarten programs. [6] On the other hand, there are 63,436 students in private daycares and pre-schools. It is possible that most of these are from families with above-average incomes.

Georgia has a long-running state-funded universal prekindergarten program now enrolling 59% of the state's four-year-olds. [7] (Private prekindergarten schools receiving state funding also use the state's curriculum.) This appears to have a strikingly positive effect on primary school learning for students in Georgia, the results for which are visible in the percentage of the state's Black children reading at grade level in grade four. While, on average, similar percentages (just under half) of White fourth graders nationally and

88

in Georgia read proficiently for their grade, higher percentages of Black fourth graders in Georgia than nationally read proficiently for that grade (22% v. 18%), which is still just half the rate for White students. Both Black and White fourth graders in Alabama read proficiently at lower rates than nationally and at much lower rates for each race than in Georgia. The percentage of Black students from more prosperous families in Georgia reading at or above grade level in fourth grade is particularly impressive: 44%, twice that of similarly situated students in Alabama and considerably higher than the national average for this group and for White students in fourth grade eligible for the National Lunch Program in either state or nationally.

School Discipline

School discipline data highlights the difference in the ways that Black children are treated by school-level authorities. It is, in effect, an indicator of racist attitudes. Out-of-school suspensions increase the likelihood that students will be required to repeat a grade and then drop out-of-school entirely. Black students in both Alabama and Georgia are dealt with more severely than White students: approximately one-fifth of all Black students receiving out-of-school suspensions; however, the racial disparity in Georgia is half that for Alabama. In 2011-12, the latest date for which information is available, 18% of Black students in Alabama were given at least one out-of-school suspension, while the figure for White students was 5.5%.[8] That year, 20% of Black students in Georgia were given at least one out-of-school suspension, while 9% of White students were given at least one out-of-school suspension. Georgia is twice as likely to remove Black students from the classroom, Alabama three times as likely to remove Black students from the classroom as they do their White students.

High School Graduation Rates and Validity

The 4-year adjusted cohort graduation rate reported by Georgia for the 2014-15 school year was 75% for Black students and 83% for White students.[9] As only 16% of Black students and 43% of White students were reading at grade level in 2011, when they were in eighth grade, and that nationally, there is only a small (one or two point) difference between eighth grade and twelfth grade achievement levels in reading, it appears that just 17% of graduating Black students in Georgia and 46% of graduating White students received their diplomas with reading skills at least at the grade 8 level.

Despite its low educational achievement levels in basic skills, the state of Alabama reports much higher than average high school graduation rates for both Black and White students. The state's 4-year adjusted cohort graduation rate for the 2014-15 school year was 87% for Black students, as compared to the national average of 75%. While nationally the average graduation rate for White students was 88%, Alabama reported a graduation rate of 91% for White students. (However, in December, 2016, Alabama's education department admitted significant inflation of graduation rates.[10]) Given that only 10% of Alabama's Black students and 34% of its White students were reading at grade level when they were in eighth grade in 2011, even if the state's reported graduation rate is accurate, it appears that only 10% of Black students in Alabama and 32% of White students graduated with reading skills at least at the grade 8 level. [11]

Of the more that three-quarters of the students in the class of 2015 who took the SAT in Georgia, just 14% of African-American SAT takers met the SAT College and Career Readiness benchmark. (Too few students in Alabama took the SAT for this indicator to be meaningful for that state.) If Black graduation rates and percentages proficient at graduation were equal to current White outcomes, each year there would be an additional 4,700 college and career ready Black high school graduates in Alabama (up from 1,700) and an additional 16,100 in Georgia (up from 5,600).

Private Schools

Private school enrollment in Alabama is disproportionately White. There are 86,000 students in private schools in Alabama, a number equal to 12% of the public school enrollment of 744,000. [12] Just 17,000 private school students are "minority," 9% of the public school enrollment of 247,300 African-American students in the state's public schools. Average tuition is $6,100 for private elementary schools and $7,100 for private high schools. Given a median family income for Black families of $35,000, a family with one child in a private elementary school and one in a private high school would have to spend more than a third of their total income on tuition.

There are fewer than 150,000 students in private schools in Georgia, compared to 1.7 million public school students. 36,000 private school students are "minority," compared to 644,000 African-American students in the state's public schools. Average tuition is $8,700 for elementary school and $10,900 for high school.[13] With an average family income for Black families of $44,000, a Black family in Georgia with one child in a private elementary school and one in a private high school would have to spend nearly half of their total income on tuition.

Three-Fifths of an Education

Focus on Atlanta

Atlanta has a majority African-American population (54%) of 224,670.[14] The racial disparities in the city are much wider than the national average, primarily because of the extraordinary levels of White educational attainment and income and the below average levels of Black income.

Atlanta					
	BA and Higher	No HS Diploma	Family Income	Unemployed	Poverty Rate
Black	21%	21%	$32,000	16%	29%
White	73%	4%	$133,00	4%	3%

Atlanta's public schools educate nearly five times the percentage of their White students as their Black students to read at grade level in the crucial eighth grade year. The National Assessment of Educational Progress results for eighth grade reading for Atlanta show that 66% of White students are proficient and above (compared to 42% nationally) as are just 14% of Black students (compared to 15% nationally). 45% of Black students in the city's public schools and 6% of White students were functionally illiterate, at NAEP's Below Basic level, in 2015.

White students, from Atlanta's more prosperous families, read at grade level 71% of the time in eighth grade. (There are too few White students from families living in or near poverty, and therefore eligible for the National Lunch Program, in the Atlanta public schools for NAEP to report.) Among Black students, educational attainment in Atlanta is sharply divided by income. Ten percent of those eligible for the National Lunch Program read at or above the proficient level, while nearly five times as many, an unusual 48% of those from more prosperous African-American families do so. A White student from a comparatively prosperous family in Atlanta is more than seven times as likely to be brought to grade level in eighth grade reading as a Black student from a low-income family. On the other hand, a Black student from a comparatively prosperous family in Atlanta is nearly as likely to read at or above grade level at eighth grade as a White student eligible for the National Lunch Program in the state of Georgia as a whole.

The latest year for which district-level school discipline data is available from the U.S. Department of Education's Office for Civil Rights is 2013-14. That year, 19% of Black students in Atlanta and 2% of White students were given at least one out-of-school suspension.[15] Teachers and school level administrators in Atlanta were ten times as likely to remove Black students from the classroom as they were to remove White students from the classroom, a disparity that has been shown to reflect adult attitudes, not student behavior.

The 4-year adjusted cohort graduation rate reported by Atlanta for the 2015-16 school year was 69% for Black students and 91% for White students (national rates were 75% for Black students and 88% for White students).[16] Given that only 12% of Atlanta's Black students and 65% of White students were reading at grade level in 2011, when they were in eighth grade, and that nationally, there is only a small (one or two point) difference between eighth grade and twelfth grade achievement levels in reading, it appears that 55-57% of graduating Black students in Atlanta and about a quarter of graduating White students received their diplomas while having serious deficiencies in their reading skills.

Three-Fifths of an Education

Focus on Alabama

An obvious point at which to begin improvements in the quality and equity in education is spending on education. The United States has a three-part system of funding for education: local (usually, but not always, from property taxes), state (from general revenue), and federal (usually for "special needs" districts and students). Federal expenditures reaching school districts are relatively small. Local and state education expenditures support varying proportions of the great majority of school spending. Local spending reflects school district resources and decisions (which often move in unison); state spending reflects state resources and decisions (the latter of which can be highly political); decisions about federal expenditures on education are political and not otherwise directly related to resources.

While total national average per pupil spending is $11,000, in 2014 Alabama districts, on average, spent $9,000. The difference could well pay for an additional teacher in each classroom.[17] Alabama *state* funding for districts is fairly uniform, around $5,500 per student. Nonetheless, total expenditure per student in Alabama varies widely, due, on the one hand, to variations in federal support, which is higher for lower-income districts and, on the other hand, variations in local tax revenues, which tend to be greater in higher-income districts. While top-spending school districts in the state exceed $12,000 per pupil, the lowest-spending district spends about $7,536: just over two-thirds, 69%, of the national average.[18] The districts with the lowest per student expenditure have local tax revenues available for education even less than those amounts provided by the Federal government. In contrast, Homewood, for example, in suburban Birmingham, which is 80% White, with a median family income of over $70,000, spends $12,719 per student: local revenue approximately matching funding from the state, with minimal federal funding.

With its overall low levels of spending on education, it is not surprising that the average pupil-to-teacher ratio in Alabama is 17.4 to 1, as compared to 15 to 1 in the neighboring states of Louisiana, Mississippi and South Carolina (and 12 to 1 in New Jersey). Another consequence of the low level of funding for education is that average starting salaries for public school teachers in Alabama are just

$36,198, which would qualify the children of those teachers for free- or reduced-priced school lunches, that indicator of low incomes.[19] Average salaries in Alabama for teachers at all levels of experience and education are just under $48,000, considerably below the median income for White families in the state. And yet wealthy Homewood City Schools teacher salaries begin at $40,000 and average $58,000, with some highly qualified teachers earning over $70,000. Alabama districts with lower local tax revenues have correspondingly lower beginning and average teacher salaries than state-wide averages, and salaries considerably lower than those available to teachers in comparatively wealthy, predominately White, school districts such as Homewood.

In 2015, Augenblick, Palaich and Associates (ABA), a Colorado-based consulting firm, produced a study of *Equity and Adequacy in Alabama Schools and Districts*. ABA found that "Over the past seven years, Alabama's school finance system has either barely met . . . or failed to meet generally accepted equity standards, and has become more inequitable."[20] ABA further found that Alabama's school finance system was relatively "inequitable in 2006-07, and that the system has worsened since then . . .

> The range between the lowest- and highest-spending districts in 2006-07 was $5,039 per student, with a ratio of 1.83 from highest to lowest. This means that, per student, the highest-spending district had over $5,000 more in financial resources than the lowest-spending district. To provide some context, this translates to $125,975 more for a classroom of 25 students – enough to pay for nearly three additional teachers at the statewide average teacher salary. This range increased to $5,509 in 2011-12 and to $6,025 in 2012-13. The ratio of the highest- to lowest-spending district also increased, to 1.92 in 2011-12 and to 2.0 in 2012-13. These increases indicate that the highest-spending district spent almost exactly twice as much per student as the lowest-spending district."[21]

From this ABA concluded that "The districts in the highest quintile have 3.4 teachers more per 1,000 students in 2012-13 than those in the lowest quintile . . . the average teacher salary in the highest

95

quintile, \$48,309, is \$1,576 higher than the average salary in the lowest quintile. This suggests that higher-wealth– and higher-spending–districts have the ability to hire more teachers and to pay them higher, more competitive salaries than poorer districts."[22]

The Augenblick, Palaich and Associates report did not consider race, but given the difference in median family incomes between Black and White families in Alabama, it would not be unjustified to substitute racial for wealth terms in the final sentence above, giving this: "This suggests that (some) White districts have the ability to hire more teachers and to pay them higher, more competitive salaries than (predominately) Black districts." Intuitively, this would have an effect on student learning. In support of this intuition, Raj Chetty and his colleagues find that "students assigned to higher [value added] teachers are more successful in many dimensions.

> They are more likely to attend college, earn higher salaries, live in better neighborhoods, and save more for retirement. They are also less likely to have children as teenagers. Teachers have large impacts in all the grades we analyze (4 to 8). Teachers' impacts on earnings are also similar in percentage terms for students from low and high income families . . .[23]

It is not unlikely that there are more of those Chetty calls "higher value-added teachers" in districts that provide higher salaries. As in Alabama these are more likely to be districts with predominately White students from higher income families, the racially and economically differentiated student achievement in Alabama schools is not a surprising, nor an accidental, outcome.

Alabama enrolls 19,400 Black students in eighth grade. Of those, 2,100 (11%) read at or above grade level. The state thereby adds about 17,000 Black students each year to its population with little chance of readiness for college or middle-income careers, little chance for economic mobility, a greater chance for incarceration, serious health problems and pre-mature death. Poor educational attainment leads to poverty, which, in turn, in the absence of state action, leads to poor educational attainment in the
next generation.

Louisiana

We turn now to the remaining former slave states in the deep south, Louisiana to the west of Georgia and Alabama and South Carolina to the east.

Louisiana has a unique history, legal system, culture and demographic mixture. It has one of the higher percentages of African-American residents (32%) and a Black population of 1,500,00.[24] While family incomes of all racial/ethnic groups in the state are below the national averages, those for Black families are even lower, less than half the state's average for White, non-Hispanic, families. A third of the Black workforce is unemployed, a third of Black residents live in poverty, a quarter of Black adults did not finish high school. While the state's White population has a standard of living near that of most White Americans; the state's Black population has a standard of living hardly recognizable as American.

The state has two metropolitan areas: New Orleans and Baton Rouge. The average Black student in the New Orleans metropolitan area attends a school in which 86% of the students are poor and where the Brown University Index of Dissimilarity, a measure of segregation, is 63, where a value of 60 is considered very high. The average Black student in the Baton Rouge metropolitan area attends a school in which 82% of the students are poor and where the Index of Dissimilarity is 70. It is the responsibility of the state's education authorities to distribute resources so as to overcome these barriers.

Educational Achievement

Louisiana is one of the few states with universal access to prekindergarten, a set of programs in this case focused on children from low-income families. A third of its 4-year olds are enrolled in

97

prekindergarten programs: half of Black children in this age group and 40% of White 4-year-olds. An evaluation of one of the programs, LA 4, has found that it "has produced a consistent pattern of significant benefits for children from low-income families for four successive cohorts.

> These benefits extend through 4th grade (the highest grade for which data are available) . . . Since achievement levels in 3rd and 4th grade are highly predictive of later academic performance and high school completion, LA 4 participants are expected to continue to perform at significantly higher levels than peers who did not have a full year of high quality Pre-K. Despite these positive outcomes, the performance of low-income LA 4 children still is below that of children from more economically advantaged families, suggesting that a one-year program may not suffice to completely overcome the income achievement gap (although the magnitude of gap reduction is about 50%). Accordingly, starting earlier to provide strong educational supports for low-income children may produce even greater lasting benefits.[25]

At fourth grade, Louisiana's public school students whose family incomes makes them eligible for the National Lunch Program in 2015 read at the national average for such children. This is a notable change from earlier years, when, as recently as the 2013 NAEP test administration, there was a five-point gap, with Louisiana's National Lunch Program eligible students at 15% proficient or above, as compared to the national figure of 20%. Nonetheless, even though students from more prosperous Louisiana families have not reached the national average proficiency for that group, there is a large income-based gap in reading proficiency at fourth grade in Louisiana as well as nationally, with the proficiency rate for higher income children double that of children from lower-income families.

Educational achievement in middle school in Louisiana varies by race. Nearly three times as many of Louisiana's White students as Black students read at grade level in the crucial grade 8 school year. Nearly half of Black students in the state (as compared to less than a quarter of White students) were at the Below Basic level for grade 8 reading in 2015. For most career, further education and citizenship purposes, students reading at the NAEP Below Basic level are functionally illiterate and have little chance of improving those skills by the time they leave school.

Student educational attainment in Louisiana is divided by family income as well as by race. Only a quarter of Louisiana's White students from families living in or near poverty, and therefore eligible for the National Lunch Program, read at grade level (proficient or above) in eighth grade, while more than a third of other White students, those from more prosperous families, read at grade level in grade 8. Among Black students in Louisiana, just 10% of those eligible for the National Lunch Program read at or above the proficient level, while twice as many, 21%, of those from more prosperous families do so. A Black student from a family with an income above the cut-off for the National Lunch Program in Louisiana is twice as likely to read at grade level as an eligible Black student. The income/achievement gap is approximately the same size for White students.

A White student from a comparatively prosperous family in Louisiana is about four times as likely to be brought by their teachers to grade level in eighth grade reading than is a Black student from a low-income family. A Black student from a comparatively prosperous family in Louisiana is nearly as likely to read at or above grade level at eighth grade as a White student eligible for the National Lunch Program. The difference between reading proficiency even of White students from comparatively prosperous families (45%) and the national average for the group (54%) is notable and is, perhaps, an indication of a systemic failure of Louisiana's public school system to adequately educate children of either race and any family income level.

The latest year for which state-level school discipline data is available from the U.S. Department of Education's Office for Civil Rights is 2011-12. That year, 14% of Black students in Louisiana and less than half that percentage, 6%, of White students were given at least one out-of-school suspension.[26] More than half of Louisiana's public school districts allow the paddling and spanking of students, often by male administrators on female students.

Three-Fifths of an Education

Research has shown that school discipline rates are in large part determined by racial attitudes of teachers and administrators and that higher rates of out-of-school suspensions and expulsions are associated with repeated grades and failure to graduate from high school.

The 4-year adjusted cohort graduation rate reported by Louisiana for the 2014-15 school year was 71% for Black students and 83% for White students (national rates were 74.6% for Black students and 87.6% for White students).[27] Given that only 12% of Black students and 32% of White students were reading at grade level in 2011, when they were in eighth grade, and that nationally, there is only a small (one or two point) difference between eighth grade and twelfth grade achievement levels in reading, it appears that just 12% of Black students in Louisiana and only a third of White students graduate with adequate reading skills.

Private Schools

An unusually high, fifteen percent, of school-age children, 130,000 students, are in private schools in Louisiana.[*] Among those, 27,000 private school students in the state are "minority" (21%), compared to 54% African-American students in the state's public schools. Average tuition is $5,800 for private elementary schools and $6,500 for private high school students in the state. Given an average income for Black families in Louisiana of $33,000, an African-American family with one child in a private elementary school and one in a private high school would have to spend more than one-third of their total income on tuition. It is clear that the prevalence of private schools in Louisiana contributes to the segregation of the public schools.

Vouchers

In 2012, then Louisiana Governor Piyush "Bobby" Jindal expanded an experiment known as the Louisiana Scholarship Program (LSP). Children attending public schools rated below average can enter a lottery for LSP vouchers providing tuition at eligible private schools of their choice. As the average voucher paid the private school $5,311 per year and the average cost of the public schools from state and local sources was $8,605, the voucher program resulted in a 38% savings for the state for participating students.* This was a good thing for a governor determined to reduce expenditures. But was it a good thing for the subjects of the experiment, those children, most of whom were Black, whose family incomes were low enough to qualify them for LSP vouchers? Would educational outcomes for these children improve if the already low funding for their education were reduced by more than one-third?

Given the legal requirement that the LSP voucher could not exceed state funding for public schools in the area, not all private schools applied to the program. As a matter of fact, the program served a quite specific group. Participating LSP schools, when compared to other private schools, were more likely to be affiliated with the Catholic church, more likely to serve Black students, and more likely to have had sharp declines in enrollment before joining the program. Not to put too fine a point on it, the Louisiana Scholarship Program is a way to use state money to support failing, mainly Catholic, private schools, while reducing support for public education, particularly those schools serving Black students from impoverished families.

Does the LSP improve the education of students receiving the vouchers and therefore having a choice of schools they wish to attend? Or, in other words, what happens to children who are deliberately sent to failing schools and have the amounts spent on their educations reduced by more than one-third? In order to answer this question, a National Bureau of Economic Research paper carefully examined the Louisiana Scholarship Program. The researchers, Atila Abulkadiroglu of Duke University, Parag A. Pathak of MIT and Christopher Walters of UC Berkeley, found that "LSP participation substantially reduces academic achievement." To be specific:

> Attendance at an LSP-eligible private school lowers math scores by 0.4 standard deviations and increases the likelihood of a

failing score by 50 percent. Voucher effects for reading, science and social studies are also negative and large. The negative impacts of vouchers are consistent across income groups, geographic areas, and private school characteristics, and are larger for younger children (NBER Working Paper No. 21839).

The research of Abulkadiroglu, Pathak and Walters tells us that giving impoverished Black students less funding for their education and placing them in failing private schools does not improve their educational opportunities. Perhaps the state should try increasing educational funding for students from impoverished families and placing them in successful schools. We know that would be helpful, just as the researchers involved with the Tuskegee Study knew that penicillin would have helped the Black men they watched die.

Is that comparison in bad taste? Too melodramatic? The high mortality and incarceration rates of badly educated, impoverished, Black Louisianans, indicates otherwise.

Conclusion

In 2003 a third of White students in Louisiana's eighth grade classes scored at or above proficient on the NAEP reading test, six points below the national average. That year, just 9% of the state's Black eight graders could read at grade level, according to NAEP, three points below the then national average for Black students. In 2015, Louisiana's White students fell further behind the national average, just 32% reading at grade level—ten points lower than the national average—and 12% of Black students, again 3 points below the national average for Black students, read at grade level in eighth grade. The White students had lost ground both absolutely and relatively; the state's Black students had improved slightly, but not relative to national averages. And the racial gap remained enormous: nearly 90% of the state's Black students could not read at grade level; over 40% had difficulty reading at all.

Nearly two-thirds of Louisiana's public school students, Black and White, who read at grade level in eighth grade have parents with at least some college education. Among other students in the state, just 10% of Black students and 27% of White students from low-income, less well-educated, families read proficiently in middle school. It is quite possible that this reflects differences in the quality of schools available to low-income Black and White students in Louisiana.

Louisiana's spending on education in relation to personal income (a measure of effort) placed it at 30th in the nation, well below other states in the region.[*] (Black Belt states South Carolina and Georgia ranked 12th and 13th, respectively.) Louisiana's per pupil expenditure in 2014 ranked 26th at $10,749, compared to a national average of $11,009.[*] This compares well with other states in the region, but quite poorly in comparison to high achieving states such as Connecticut ($17,700) and New Jersey ($17,900). The average salary for teachers in Louisiana is $51,000 (average beginning salary is $39,000).[*] These salaries are far below the average income of White families in the state. Perhaps if teacher salaries were sufficient to support a middle class standard of living more highly qualified people would be attracted to teaching in Louisiana and student achievement results would be better.

If Black graduation rates and percentages proficient at graduation were equal to current White outcomes, each year there would be an additional 5,600 college- and career-ready Black high school graduates in Louisiana (up from the estimated current 1,500).

Each year, Louisiana enrolls about 24,000 Black students in eighth grade. Of those, 3,600 are taught to read at or above grade level. The state, then, adds over 20,000 Black students each year to its population with little chance of readiness for college or middle income careers, little chance for economic mobility, a greater chance for incarceration, serious health problems and pre-mature death.

Three-Fifths of an Education

South Carolina

South Carolina was, in effect, settled by enslaved West Africans brought to the "low country" along the coast to use their traditional skills to raise indigo and rice. Three centuries later the state has nearly double the national average percentage of African-American residents (28%), and one of the larger Black populations in terms of absolute numbers (1.3 million). The descendants of enslaved Africans now living in South Carolina continue to suffer from the effects of slavery and lingering Jim Crow. The median Black family income is less than three-fifths of that of White, non-Hispanic, South Carolina families. More of the state's Black residents have not finished high school (19%) than have graduated from college (15%). The percentage of White college graduates is double that of the percentage of the state's Black college graduates. Forty percent of school-age Black children in the South Carolina live in poverty.

Forty-two percent of the state's African-American households, more than twice the national average percentage for all Americans, are in the bottom fifth of the national income distribution and only 7% have incomes in the top fifth of the national income distribution. Nowhere in South Carolina are a child's chances of reaching that top fifth of the national income distribution given parents with incomes in the bottom fifth greater than 5%. That is the average for all state residents. It is, of course, worse for South Carolina's African-American residents. Unless there is a change in the state's education system, things will stay that way.

Educational Achievement

South Carolina enrolls 40% of its 4-year-olds in state-supported prekindergarten programs, which should be a good thing. The National Institute for Early Education Research ranks it 12th among the states for access to pre-school. But it ranks only 35th for resources provided to prekindergartens. High quality early childhood education programs have been shown to have positive effects on primary school learning. However, in South Carolina, with its deficient funding of prekindergarten, by fourth grade most African-American students in the state's public schools are assessed by the National Assessment of Educational Progress as functionally illiterate (Below Basic) and just 15% have the expected reading skills for that grade. The comparable percentages for the state's White students are reversed: 45% reading proficiently and just 22% with skills that are judged as Below Basic.

The state's White, non-Hispanic, fourth-graders, whether from lower- or middle-income families, read at the national averages for each group. Black fourth-graders from lower-income families, that is, most Black families, have lower achievement levels than the national average for lower-income Black children. On the other hand, fourth-graders from the state's minority of middle income Black families have higher achievement levels than the national average for their group. The state's Black-White gap for lower-income student is 19 percentage points in favor of White students among those students reading at grade level, while among middle income students the gap is a virtually identical 20 percentage points in favor of White students at the proficient and above level. Black students are more than twice as likely as White students to be left functionally illiterate by their schools by fourth grade and only a third as likely to be taught to read proficiently.

The educational opportunities in the primary grades in South Carolina are clearly differentiated by race at each rung of the family income ladder.

By eighth grade, the percentage (48%) of South Carolina's Black students who are functionally illiterate has declined slightly from the level at fourth grade, but so has the percentage (11%) reading at grade level. The White-Black gap is 27 percentage points among proficient readers and the Black-White gap is 31 percentage points among those assessed as reading Below Basic, both gaps having widened after four years of schooling. More than half of the state's Black students from lower-income families are functionally illiterate at grade eight, as are nearly a third of Black students from middle-income families. While 23% of Black students from middle-income families read at grade level, only a negligible 9% of those Black students from lower-income families have been taught to be proficient readers by eighth grade. A White, non-Hispanic, student in middle school from a lower-income family is more likely to read proficiently than a Black student from a middle income family and less likely to have been left functionally illiterate by their school. A White student in South Carolina whose parents did not finish high school is more likely to be taught by their school to read proficiently than a Black child of college graduates. Having college-educated parents gives White students in South Carolina a 27 percentage point advantage over those with parents without a high school diploma, but the gap between Black students with college-educated parents and those with only a high school education is just two percentage points.

One explanation for these differences in educational opportunities might be found in the continuing racial segregation of the schools in South Carolina. According to data from Brown University's US Schools research program, in the Charleston metropolitan area, where half the students are white and over one-third are Black, a White elementary school student is likely to be in a school where two-thirds of the other students are White, while a Black elementary student will be in a school that where over half the other students are Black. And the average Black student will be in a school that is 62% poor, regardless of the income level of that student's own family. Racial and income segregation are slightly more severe in the state's other metropolitan area, that around the state capitol of Columbia.

School discipline practices are another factor restricting educational opportunities in South Carolina, as elsewhere. The latest year for which state-level school discipline data is available from the U.S. Department of Education's Office for Civil Rights is 2011-12. That year, 17% of Black students in South Carolina and less than half that percentage, 7%, of White students were given at least one out-of-school suspension. Research has shown that school discipline rates are in large part determined by racial attitudes of teachers and administrators and that higher rates of out-of-school suspensions and expulsions are associated with repeated grades and failure to graduate from high school.

Private Schools

There are 411 private schools in South Carolina, enrolling 65,700 students. The percentage of minority students in the state's private schools is less than one-third that of the percentage of minority students in the state's public schools. Elementary school tuition averages $8,800; high school tuition averages $6,600.[*] Given an average income for Black families in South Carolina of $38,500, an African-American family with one child in a private elementary school and one in a private high school would have to spend 40% of their total income on tuition. In other words, the state's private schools disproportionately serve White families and tend to increase segregation in the public schools.

The educational opportunities available in South Carolina's schools culminate with (or without) high school graduation. The 4-year adjusted cohort graduation rate reported by South Carolina for the 2014-15 school year was 77% for Black students and 83% for White students. Given that only 11% of Black students and 38% of White students in South Carolina were reading at grade level in 2011, when they were in eighth grade, it appears that just 12% of Black students in ninth grade four years later graduate with adequate reading skills. This estimate is supported by the fact that just 9% of African-American students in South Carolina who took the SAT in 2015 met the College Board's College and Career Readiness Benchmark. And, of course, not all students take the SAT. (The SAT College and Career Readiness rate for White students in the state was at least four times that of African-American students.) It is, then, unsurprising that nearly twice the percentage of White as Black South Carolina students beginning high school go on to earn a college degree.

108

If Black graduation rates and percentages proficient at graduation were equal to current White outcomes. If this goal were reached, each year there would be an additional 6,400 college- and career-ready Black high school graduates in South Carolina (up from the estimated current 1,500).

Conclusion

South Carolina no longer has legally segregated schools, but its schools remain largely segregated by race and doubly so by income. The result is that although nearly a quarter of Black students from middle income families in the state are taught to read at the expected level in middle school, fewer than a tenth of Black students from lower-income families are taught to read proficiently and half are left functionally illiterate. And even those Black students from middle income families are only half as likely to be taught to read proficiently as are their White peers and nearly a third of them are left functionally illiterate. South Carolina's Black citizens remain in the situation defined for them by the Founders at three-fifths of the level of their White neighbors.

Three-Fifths of an Education

North Carolina

In some ways and places North Carolina follows the traditions of Jim Crow racism, while in others, it is building a technology-oriented, racially integrated society exemplified by the Research Triangle in the Raleigh-Durham-Chapel Hill area. North Carolina has an above average percentage of African-American residents (22%), and one of the larger Black populations in terms of absolute numbers (2,170,000). A few counties, primarily in the north-eastern part of the state, have a majority lower-income Black population. The counties in the far west, Appalachian region, are almost entirely White, non-Hispanic, under-educated and impoverished.

The state's Black residents are less likely to graduate from either high school or college or even to enroll in its better-known universities than its White, non-Hispanic, residents. The University of North Carolina has a Black enrollment of only 8%; the Black enrollment of private Duke University is 10%, the African-American undergraduate enrollment of North Carolina State is just 6%: in each case far below the proportion of the state's Black college-age population. Black family incomes are only two-thirds of those of White families, their unemployment rate is more than double and their poverty rate is almost triple that of their White neighbors. The largest occupational group for White residents of the state is management, business, science and the arts; that for Black residents is service occupations, as is traditional in this state and many others.

North Carolina once had a reputation as one of the more progressive, if not the most progressive, of southern states. That has changed. The Republican majority in the state legislature has refused to cooperate with the new Democratic governor, changing rules and laws to transfer traditional gubernatorial powers to the legislature, removing their opponents from state and local offices, and making

111

repeated efforts to racially gerrymander electoral districts, despite court challenges. It has also reduced funding for public schools and universities, while promoting vouchers and private charter schools.

It is a commonplace of historical research that the destruction of post-Civil War democratic reforms was partly accomplished by the creation of race-based politics. Impoverished White farmers were persuaded to vote against their own economic interests, ending a nascent inter-racial populist movement. Today, there are twice as many lower-income White families as there are lower-income Black families in the state, and yet the dominant political faction in North Carolina has persuaded White voters to vote against measures to improve their own lot with the argument that such measures might also improve that of Black residents. For example, in the recent election for governor, the overwhelmingly White, impoverished Appalachian counties of the state voted for the candidate running on a platform of shifting state funding for education from their public schools to charter and private fee-charging schools.

Educational Achievement

The National Institute for Early Education Research ranks North Carolina 25th among the states for access to prekindergarten and 19th for the resources committed to pre-school. As a result, 80% of the state's 4-year-olds cannot find spaces in North Carolina's prekindergarten program, a percentage that has not improved in nearly a decade. State funding per child enrolled declined from $8,000 in 2002 to 5,300 in 2016.

Two-thirds of the state's White, non-Hispanic, families have incomes higher than the eligibility requirement for the National Lunch Program, $45,000, but only 40% of the state's Black families have such middle class incomes. Nineteen percent of students from the majority of Black families who are lower-income and 44% of middle class Black students are taught to read proficiently in fourth grade, as are 36% of lower-income White, non-Hispanic, students and nearly two-thirds of the majority middle class White students. All of these outcomes are substantially higher than national averages, with particularly large improvements for Black students from middle class families able to afford private preschools for their children.

These results are, however, strongly indicative of both racial- and income-based differences in educational opportunities, overall White achievement levels being more than twice as high as those of Black students, and both within and across racial categories, middle class achievement levels are twice as high as those of students from lower-income families

By middle school most of these primary school achievement levels have declined to below national averages and the racial gaps have widened. North Carolina middle schools give more than three times as many of their White students (40%) as their Black students (13%) the opportunity to read at grade level in the crucial eighth grade year. In that grade, White students from families living in or near poverty, and therefore eligible for the National Lunch Program, read at grade level (proficient or above) 26% of the time, twice that of average Black students, while other White students, from more prosperous families, read at grade level twice again as often yet. Among Black students, just 9% of those eligible for the National Lunch Program read at or above the proficient level, while more than three times as many, 31%, of those from more prosperous families do so, a particularly dramatic income-based difference.

There are great geographical differences in household income across the state, with higher income households concentrated in the center of the state, in Wake, Chatham and Durham counties, while lower-income households are to be found in the Appalachian region and the northeastern counties, the former with predominately White populations, the latter predominately Black. Durham County, which is 38% Black and a technology and research center (with well-integrated schools), has an average household income of $52,000 per year, while Halifax County, which is 53% Black, has an average household income of $32,000 and Appalachian Graham County, which is 88% White, has an average household income of $34,000. A White student from a comparatively prosperous family in, for example, Wake County or the Charlotte area, is more than five times as likely to be brought to grade level in eighth grade reading than a Black student from a lower-income family anywhere in the state. A Black student from a comparatively prosperous family in the

Research Triangle area is much more likely to read at or above grade level at eighth grade than a White student eligible for the National Lunch Program in Appalachia.

In other words, educational opportunities in North Carolina vary first by race, then by income, both powerfully affecting student learning achievement.

In general, since the turn of the century, educational outcomes for students in North Carolina have worsened or not improved for students from lower-income families and become better for middle class students. In 2002, 32% of lower-income White, non-Hispanic, students in eighth grade scored at the proficient or above level on the NAEP reading test. By 2015 that percentage had declined to 25%. Meanwhile, the percentage of White students from middle class families scoring at that level had increased from 44% to 50%. Black students from lower-income families had scored at the 9% proficient and above level in 2002 and also in 2015, while the percentage of Black students from middle class families in eighth grade reading proficiently had risen from 18% in 2002 to 31% in 2015. Educational opportunities for lower-income students in North Carolina, Black and White, have declined or failed to improve and those for lower-income Black students have remained hardly existent. The dramatic improvement for middle class Black students has taken place only in the last two NAEP assessments. In 2011 the percentage of middle class Black students who were proficient in reading stood at 23%. It then rose to 33% in 2013, before settling back slight to 31%. This is quite remarkable. It will be interesting to find if this extraordinary occurrence holds in the next assessment. In the meantime, if it does hold up, it appears to be attributable to outcomes for Black students whose parents were college graduates, the percentage of whom testing as proficient jumped from 25% to 39% between 2011 and 2015. The 31% of those reading proficiently—middle class children of college graduates—amount to just 7% of the Black children in eighth grade: 1,700 out of 31,400 students.

As is common across the country, school disciplinary actions taken by teachers and administrators often depend on the race of the student. The latest year for which state-level school discipline data is available from the U.S. Department of Education's Office for Civil

Rights is 2011-12. That year, 17% of Black students in North Carolina and just 5% of White students were given at least one out-of-school suspension, which is a measure not so much of differences in student behavior as of discriminatory attitudes of school staffs.

Graduation Rates

The 4-year adjusted cohort graduation rate reported by North Carolina for the 2014-15 school year was 82% for Black students and 88% for White students (national rates were 74.6% for Black students and 87.6% for White students). Given the percentages of students who were reading at grade level in 2011, when they were in eighth grade, and that nationally, there is only a small (one or two point) difference between eighth grade and twelfth grade achievement levels in reading, it appears that nearly 90% of graduating Black students in North Carolina and more than half of graduating White students received their diplomas while having serious deficiencies in their reading skills. This is substantiated by the finding of the College Board that just 12% of African-American SAT takers in the class of 2015 met the SAT College and Career Readiness Benchmark, as compared to a state average of 40%. Just over half of Black students from the class of 2015 took the test. We can assume that the great preponderance of those were college-bound Black seniors, which supports an estimate of adequately educated Black high school graduates as less than 10% of their cohort. If North Carolina's Black students graduated from high school college- and career-ready at the same rate as the state's White students, there would be 14,000 more well educated Black high school graduates in North Carolina each year, added to the current total of 3,000.

Three-Fifths of an Education

Focus: Charlotte

Charlotte, North Carolina's largest city, has an African-American population of 96,000, comprising slightly more than one-third (35%) of the city's residents.[28] They are more highly educated and have a higher median family income than the national average for African-Americans. White residents exceed national averages for White, non-Hispanics, in these categories by an even greater extent.

Place	BA and Higher	No HS Diploma	Family Income	Unemployed	Poverty Rate
Black					
Charlotte	23%	15%	$54,500	13%	17%
U.S.	20%	15%	$45,000	11%	25%
White					
Charlotte	50%	8%	$119,000	7%	6%
U.S.	32%	11%	$73,000	5%	12%

The National Assessment of Educational Progress results for eighth grade reading for Charlotte show that Charlotte's public schools educate more than three times the percentage of their White students as their Black students to read at grade level in the crucial eighth grade year: 58% of White students are proficient and above (compared to 42% nationally) as are 18% of Black students (compared to 15% nationally). Over one-third, 37%, of Black students in the city's public schools, but only 8% of White students were at the Below Basic level in 2015.

Student educational attainment in Charlotte, as in the rest of the state, is sharply divided by income. Although there are too few White students from families living in or near poverty, and therefore eligible for the National Lunch Program, in the Charlotte public schools for NAEP to report its test results, other White students, from more prosperous families, read at grade level 64% of the time in eighth grade. Among Black students, 14% of those eligible for the

National Lunch Program read at or above the proficient level, while nearly three times as many, 37%, of those from more prosperous families do so. A White student from a comparatively prosperous family in Charlotte is four and five times as likely to be brought to grade level in eighth grade reading as a Black student from a low-income family. A Black student from a comparatively prosperous family in Charlotte is much more likely to read at or above grade level at eighth grade than a White student eligible for the National Lunch Program in the state of North Carolina as a whole.

The latest year for which district-level school discipline data is available from the U.S. Department of Education's Office for Civil Rights is 2013-14. That year, 15% of Black students in Charlotte and 3% of White students were given at least one out-of-school suspension.[29] In other words, Charlotte's teachers and school-level administrators are five times as likely to exclude a Black student from the classroom as they are to exclude a White student. This disproportionality in school discipline has been shown to be a measure of school employees' racial attitudes.

The 4-year adjusted cohort graduation rate reported by Charlotte for the 2015-16 school year was 90% for Black students and 95% for White students (national rates were 74.6% for Black students and 87.6% for White students).[30] Given that only 18% of Black students and 57% of White students were reading at grade level in 2011, when they were in eighth grade, and that nationally, there is only a small (one or two point) difference between eighth grade and twelfth grade achievement levels in reading, it appears that 70-72% of graduating Black students in Charlotte and nearly half of graduating White students received their diplomas while having serious deficiencies in their reading skills.

Conclusion: North Carolina

All in all, educational opportunities are getting fewer for most Black students as well as for lower-income White students in North Carolina. Perhaps as a consequence, nowhere in the state does a child with family income in the bottom 20% have more than a 6% chance of reaching the top 20% of the income distribution and in most of the state the chances are less than 5%.

The state provides White students, on average, with bench-mark educational opportunities at three times the level as those provided to Black students and hardly at all to Black students from lower-income families. The only African-American children who have anything close to the opportunities available to the average White student in the state are those who have the advantage of college-educated, middle class, parents.

Funding for public education in the state has been declining for much of the past decade and now North Carolina ranks 45th in per pupil expenditure on instruction and 48th in elementary-secondary school system finance amounts per pupil to $1,000 personal income, a measure of the state's commitment, or lack of it, to education. The state's average teacher compensation is nearly 20% less than the national average. Instead of restoring adequate funding for the public schools, the state legislature has supported expansion of charter schools, which can be private, and vouchers for tuition at private schools. Researchers at Duke University have found that the state's charter schools are highly segregated and tend to be used to remove White students from integrated public school systems, fostering the politics of racial division.

It would be good if the state legislature remembered that all children deserve the opportunity for a high quality public education, without regard to race or income, even in North Carolina.

Virginia

The long march for equality and democracy in America goes through the schoolhouse door in Virginia as much as that in any other state. The last gasp of legal Jim Crow took place in Virginia, when that state's government replied to the Supreme Court's decision in *Brown* with "massive resistance" to school integration.

Today some things have changed; some things have remained pretty much the same.

Virginia's Department of Education publishes "School Quality Profiles" on the Internet, easily searchable by school or "division" (district). These profiles include the percentage of students tested as achieving proficiency in reading, math, science and social studies. The results are impressive. For example, the Virginia Department of Education judges that 76% of eighth grade students are proficient or advanced in reading. The state breaks this down to 84% of White, non-Hispanic, students reaching the proficient or advanced level in grade 8 reading during the 2016-17 school year, as did 59% of Black students. The 25-percentage-point gap is troubling, but it would be encouraging if the state's public schools taught more than half of its Black students to read at the level expected for middle school students.

But do they?

We can perform a direct comparison at the state level between student learning as assessed and reported by the Department of Education of Virginia and the National Assessment of Educational Progress results for eighth grade reading for the state. NAEP is widely considered "the gold standard" of student assessments. If there is a difference between assessments, NAEP is to be preferred. NAEP's most recent report on grade eight reading for Virginia show that by its standard 44% of White students are proficient and above as are 16% of Black students. This indicates that Virginia's assessments at grade eight for proficiency in reading for White, non-Hispanic, students should be divided in half, those for Black students should be divided by nearly four.

We might, at this point, observe that inflating student learning achievement in this manner is not useful for the students, who are being given the impression that they have skills that half or three-quarters of them do not in fact possess; nor for educators, who look to these assessments for guidance for their efforts; nor for the state legislature and governor, who might wish to use these assessments in their budgetary and other planning. As a result of these distortions, students may have false expectations for their futures; teachers may base their lesson plans on an incorrect understanding of the tasks to be accomplished; and district administrations and boards of education, as well as the state government, may not appropriate and allocate resources effectively. As a matter of fact, in regard to how scarce resources are allocated, Virginia ranks 29th among the states in per pupil expenditures on education and 42nd on expenditures in relation to personal income. These are indications of the state's commitment, or lack of commitment, to education. Virginia shows a similar lack of investment in the provision of preschool education, for which, according to the National Institute for Early Education Research, it ranks 29th for both access and spending.

As far as educational opportunity is concerned, many schools in Virginia distribute opportunities quite inequitably to their students, basing them first on race, then in accordance with family income. In regard to race, White students are nearly three times as likely to be taught to read proficiently in Virginia's middle schools as are Black students. But, it is not enough in Virginia for a student to be White to secure a good education. It is necessary also to belong to a family that is not poor. Using the NAEP standards, we find that White students from Virginia families living in or near poverty, and therefore eligible for the National Lunch Program, read at grade level at eighth grade just 20% of the time, while other White students, from more prosperous families, read at grade level more than twice as often: 51% of the time. These inequities are compounded for

Virginia's Black students: only 12% of those eligible for the National Lunch Program read at or above the proficient level, while twice as many, 25%, of those from more prosperous families do so, which is still half the percentage of their White peers.

A White student from a comparatively prosperous family in Virginia is more than four times as likely to be brought to grade level in eighth grade reading than a Black student from a lower-income family. A Black student from a comparatively prosperous family in Virginia is more likely to read at or above grade level at eighth grade than a White student eligible for the National Lunch Program. And even an above-average family income is not sufficient to secure three-quarters of affluent Black students the opportunity to read proficiently in middle school.

Virginia has undergone enormous, and accelerating, changes in the decades since *Brown* and the state's "massive resistance" to desegregation and educational equity. It has changed from a uniformly, nearly feudal society, steeped in the heritage of slavery, to one that is highly varied, in parts still agricultural, in others technology-based with a majority of residents who have relocated from the Northeast of the United States. Educational opportunities are as variable across the state as this picture would indicate. Prince Edward County, in the south-central part of the state, closed its public schools after *Brown* rather than desegregate them. The state reports that now 43% of the reopened school district's Black students (who are 57% of enrollment) read proficiently in grade 8, which would be 11% or 12% on the NAEP scale. The state assessment is of 59% for White, non-Hispanic, students, that is, about 30% on the NAEP scale. And in Richmond, the state capitol (and former capitol of the Confederacy), the state reports that 37% of Black students (who are 71% of enrollment there) and 85% of White, non-Hispanic, students read a the proficient or advanced levels, which translate by national standards to 10% of Black students and 43% of White, non-Hispanic, students: and to 90% of Black students who don't.

On the other hand, Fairfax County, a wealthy suburb of Washington, D.C. in the northern part of the state, reports 69% of Black students (who are just 10% of its enrollment) read proficiently by state standards, which would be 19% on NAEP, and 81% of White, non-Hispanic, which would be 40% on NAEP, read at grade level.

It is, then, not unusual in Virginia for a district to fail to bring nearly 90% of its Black students to grade level proficiency in middle school by national standards, while succeeding in this fundamental task for 40% of its White, non-Hispanic, students. And it is not now unknown for schools in those parts of the state where old times are nearly forgotten to triple learning opportunities for Black students from the level where the traditions of Jim Crow survive. Black students moving from Prince Edward County or Richmond to Fairfax would nearly double their opportunity to learn to read proficiently. Moving to a suburban Virginia school system would increase the likelihood of learning to read proficiently for a middle class Black student to 30%.

Disparate educational outcomes in Virginia are facilitated by two overlapping types of segregation: racial and income. Public schools in Richmond, for example, have a Brown University Index of Dissimilarity of 69 on a scale where 60 or above is considered very highly segregated and the average Black student attends a school in which 77% of the students come from poor families and 87% are Black. On the other hand, the Fairfax County Public Schools Dissimilarity Index is just 47 and Black students typically attend schools where just 38% of their students from poor families. A reasonable hypothesis would be that differing educational opportunities for Black students between these districts follow from these differences in the intensity of racial and income segregation.

But why is it that the quality of education available to a student varies with that student's race and family income? Part of the answer is that expenditure on that student's education varies with location and the degrees of segregation found there. Schools in Virginia, as most elsewhere in the United States, are funded by a locally-based tripartite system of revenue from local, state and federal sources. In Virginia, state funding is higher for districts with lower amounts of local funding (and, as elsewhere, federal funding varies with poverty levels and other special needs). In Prince Edward County, per pupil expenditure totals $11,300 per year, more than half of which comes from the state, partially compensating for the very low $3,800 per year from local resources. In Fairfax County, per pupil expenditure totals $14,200 per year, more than 25% higher than that provided to Prince Edward County students. $10,400 of this comes from local sources (close to the total of Prince Edward County's expenditure), with just $3,200 from state sources and a negligible amount from federal sources.

Investment in a Black student's education increases by a quarter if that student moves from Prince Edward County to Fairfax County, both racial and income segregation dramatically decrease and, according to Raj Chetty's Equality of Opportunity Project, that student's chances of reaching the top 20% of income distribution, given parents in the bottom 20%, doubles.

Why should total investments in a student's education, in this increasingly wealthy state, vary with the amount of local taxation revenues? Equalizing per student expenditures across the state to at least the level of Fairfax County would be a major step toward improving educational achievement for Virginia's students who are the descendants of enslaved Africans, many of whom would have been brought from Africa and sold into slavery by Virginia-based slave traders, sold, as often as not, in Richmond, while being displayed to prospective buyers and random gawkers like cattle.

Another factor restricting educational opportunities for Black students in Virginia is the racial attitudes of some school staff. This can be seen in school discipline data. Research has convincingly shown that disciplinary actions by school-level staff, such as out-of-school suspensions, are much more dependent on the racial attitudes of teachers and school administrators than on the activities of students. The latest year for which state-level school discipline data is available from the U.S. Department of Education's Office for Civil Rights is 2011-12. In that year, 5% of White students and three times that proportion, 14%, of Black students in Virginia and were given at least one out-of-school suspension. (This is quite close to the 16% figure for Black adults in Virginia who have not completed high school and, perhaps coincidentally, the 16% percentage of African-Americans in Virginia who live in poverty.) Throwing a student out of class often begins the process by which that student is prevented from completing their education.

Unequal educational opportunities in k-12 schooling in Virginia culminate in large numbers of Black students being denied high school diplomas. The 4-year adjusted cohort graduation rate reported by the state for the 2014-15 school year was 79% for Black students, but 90% for White students. (The graduation rate of Black students in the Richmond schools is 69%, that of White students 90%. In Fairfax those rates are 82% and 95%, respectively.) Given that only 16% of Black students and 44% of White students were reading at grade level in 2011, when they were in eighth grade, it appears that 80% of graduating Black students in Virginia and more than half of graduating White students received their diplomas while having serious deficiencies in their reading skills. This is borne out by the fact that just 17% of those African-American students who took the SAT in 2015—and only college-bound students would take that test—met the SAT College and Career Readiness Benchmark. If Black students in Virginia were educated to the same extent as White, non-Hispanic, students, 10,000 rather than the current 3,000 would graduate each year college- and career-ready.

It is not "natural" that the allocation of resources should vary from district to district within Virginia—or any other state—depending on local tax revenues. More equitable systems are not beyond the keen of human intelligence. Nor is it "natural"—must one say this?—that educational opportunities should be greater for middle class White students than for Black students from lower-income families. It is good that one or two Virginia school districts and some suburbs offer greater educational opportunities for African-American students than are offered elsewhere in the state, even if these are simply the by-products for relatively small minorities of Black students of increased investments in the educations of upper-middle class White children. It is good to take symbolic steps to erase the vestiges of slavery and Jim Crow. However, a decision by the governor of Virginia, and its legislature, is needed to change the state's education system, root and branch, so that educational opportunities are not determined by the color of a student's skin, by the size of a student's parents' bank account, by the location of that student's school. Until the state's governor and the state legislature do these things, the responsibility for the lack of educational opportunities for the descendants of enslaved Africans in Virginia remains theirs.

Three-Fifths of an Education

Florida

Florida, Texas and California each have large Black populations and larger Hispanic populations.

Florida, a former slave state, was a member of the Confederacy, an adherent of Jim Crow and a resister of school desegregation. More Black people were lynched, per capita, in Florida than in any other state. It has a percentage of African-American residents (16%), just over the national average, and one of the larger Black populations in terms of absolute numbers (3.3 million). Unlike similar neighboring states, it also has a large and varied Hispanic population (4.5 million). Half of Florida's Hispanics are first-generation immigrants, as are 20% of Florida's Black population, an unusual proportion.[31] While nationally, median Black and Hispanic family incomes are similar, in Florida that of Hispanic families is greater. And while nationally, Black educational attainment is considerably higher than Hispanic educational attainment, in Florida this situation, too, is reversed. This is perhaps attributable to the high proportion of Hispanics in Florida who are of Latin American origin, from nations many of which have well-developed education systems.

Florida's Black median family income is close to the national average for African-Americans (although, of course much lower than the state's median White family income), and the unemployment and poverty rates are lower, that is, better, than the national averages. On the other hand, the Black population of Florida is less well-educated than the Black population of the country as a whole, with a slightly lower percentage of Black adults having finished college and a very much larger percentage of adults not having completed high school. The White population in Florida is as likely to have completed college as the national average for that population and less likely to have left school without a high school diploma. Median White, non-Hispanic, family income in Florida is lower than that for the nation as a whole as are the unemployment and poverty rates.

But it is perhaps unwise to generalize about the state. Florida's population profile differs greatly between that in the northern part of the state, which was part of the slave economy, and the more recently populated middle and far south. Duval County, for example, in the northeast, is centered on Jacksonville, which was, and is, a port for the agricultural production of northern Florida, southern Georgia and Alabama and is culturally similar to the latter. Hillsborough County (Tampa), on the Gulf of Mexico, was a center of the Cuban-connected tobacco industry and is now a major vacation and retirement destination. And Miami-Dade has become, in effect, a, if not the, Caribbean metropolis. These differences are reflected in the fact that less than five percent of the White and Black populations and a third of the (relatively small) Hispanic population of Duval County are foreign born and 13% of the White population, 11% of the Black population, and just more than a third of the Hispanic residents of Hillsborough Country were born in other countries. In comparison, more than one million of Miami-Dade's Hispanic residents were born in other countries. (As is well-known, more than half of Miami's Hispanics are of Cuban origin.) A third of Miami residents, and 60% of its foreign-born residents, speak English less than well. The percentages of White, non-Hispanic, adults completing college is similar across these three counties, slightly less than the US average. The percentages of Black adults completing college is at the national average in Hillsborough County and below average in Duval and Miami-Dade. Fewer than the national average of Black adults have received high school diplomas in these counties. In Miami-Dade, nearly a quarter of Black adults have not completed high school.[32]

Educational Achievement: prekindergarten Effects

Florida enrolls a remarkable 76% of its 4-year-olds in that state's prekindergarten programs, giving it a rank of second in the nation for access to prekindergarten, according to the National Institute for Early Education Research. Unfortunately, state funding for these programs is not a match for that degree of access: the state ranks 40th for spending on prekindergarten and the state meets few of NIEER's "quality standards."

Despite the state's below average per student expenditure for prekindergarten, the positive effects of good access to prekindergarten are clear. In fourth grade, while neighboring Alabama has grade four reading proficiency under the national averages at just 15% for Black students and 37% for White students, Florida's Black fourth graders have a 20% chance of reading at grade level and half of their White classmates read at grade level in fourth grade. Florida's Black fourth graders who are eligible for the National Lunch Program read at the national average for similar Black students and thus are more likely than their Alabama peers to read at grade level in fourth grade, while their classmates from more prosperous Black families are close to the national average of that group and 40% more likely than economically similar students in Alabama to reach or exceed grade level reading proficiency. But Duval County, the culturally "Southernmost" of the three metropolitan area school districts for which this data is available, has lower percentages of both Black and White children in public prekindergarten classes than the state average. It therefore unsurprisingly lags the others and the state in supporting reading proficiency in grade four both for those students eligible for the National Lunch Program and for those from more prosperous families. It does less well for Black students, in general, and particularly for those Black students from lower-income families.

Educational Achievement: Eighth Grade Reading

Both Black and White, non-Hispanic, students in Florida schools reach levels of reading proficiency in eighth grade at similar rates as their national peers. As elsewhere, student educational attainment in Florida differs within race by income. Florida has a relatively small income-related gap among its Black students, due to a slightly higher achievement level for those eligible for the National Lunch Program and a considerably lower level for those not eligible. In other words, in Florida, the balance between race and class as influences on

129

educational achievement is unusually tipped toward race. A lower-income White, non-Hispanic, student from Florida qualifying for the National Lunch Program is at least twice as likely or more to read at grade level in eighth grade than a Black student from a similarly impoverished background. And White students from middle class families are more than twice as likely to read at grade level as middle class Black students. Nearly 90% of the half of Black students eligible for the National Lunch Program in Florida (and over 90% in Hillsborough County) do not reach proficiency in grade eight reading.

School Discipline Inequities

In school year 2011-12, a fifth, 20%, of Black students in Florida were given at least one out-of-school suspension, but less than half that percentage, 9%, of White students were. (In the Dade and Duval schools, almost three times, in Hillsborough more than three times, the percentage of Black as White, non-Hispanic, students were given at least one out-of-school suspension in 2013.) These inequitable discipline policies, along with the racially-determined distribution of educational opportunities reflected in reading proficiency achievement, contribute to a low high school graduation rate for Black students.

The 4-year adjusted cohort graduation rate reported by Florida for the 2014-15 school year was a remarkably low 68% for Black students and 83% for White students. (National rates were reported as 75% and 88%, respectively.) If these rates are adjusted to include only those students who read proficiently when in eighth grade, it appears that just 19% of Black students and 44% of White students in Florida graduate with at least middle school reading skills. Just 13% of African-American students who took the SAT in 2015 met the SAT College and Career Readiness benchmark. If Black graduation rates and percentages proficient at graduation in Florida were equal to current White outcomes, each year there would be an additional 13,600 college- and career-ready Black high school graduates in Florida (up from the estimated current 4,500).

Focus: Three Florida Districts

The National Assessment of Educational Progress provides information about three Florida districts: Miami-Dade, Duval and Hillsborough. Black students in the Miami schools read at grade level in eighth grade just 16% of the time, about as often as the extraordinarily low national average, but Hispanic students are brought to proficiency in reading in eighth grade twice as often as that and half again more than the national average for Hispanic students. The district fails to bring 89% of its male Black students from lower-income families eligible for the National Lunch Program to proficiency in grade 8 reading. The Miami-Dade district, with its majority Hispanic enrollment illustrates the fallacy of grouping Black and Hispanic (and Asian and Native American) students under the rubric of "students of color." For example, Miami Northwestern High School, in the city's historic Black community, has virtually no Asian students and more than ten times as many Black as Hispanic students. "Minority," in Liberty City, "students of color," means Black. Miami Palmetto Senior High School, on the other hand, far to the south, is 60% Hispanic, 20% White, 14% Black and 4% Asian. Minority, students of color, at Miami Palmetto, means Hispanic.

These racial/ethnic differences are expressed in the district's support for students in these schools. Miami Northwestern High School (which is listed as nearly 90% economically disadvantaged by the Florida Department of Education), brings just 27% of its students to the point where they can pass the state's English Language Arts tests. The state has most recently given the school a grade of "C." (Between 1999 and 2010 the school's grades varied between "D" and "F." Between 2011 and 2014 the school's grades suddenly ran to "B's" and even "achieved" one "A," before settling on "C" in the following years). And yet the school claims a graduation rate in 2015-16 of 85%. Miami Palmetto High School, "just" 44% of the students of which are economically disadvantaged, has been rated either "A" or "B" since 2001 and 60% of its students have passed the state's English Language Arts tests. It has a reported graduation rate of 89%.[33] Despite their similar graduation rates it is clear that the comparatively prosperous students at Miami Palmetto

131

High are receiving a better education than the impoverished, racially isolated, students at Miami Northwestern.

This picture holds for the other two Florida districts for which the National Assessment of Educational Progress provides detailed information. In Duval (Jacksonville and environs), William M. Raines High School, which has a state grade of "C" and an English Language Arts Achievement score of 15%, is virtually entirely Black and 100% economically disadvantaged. (And yet it has a reported graduation rate of 92%.) Duncan U. Fletcher High School, which has a 2017 grade of "B" and an English Language Arts Achievement test passing rate four times as high (59%), is just 28% minority (predominately Hispanic) and less than a third economically disadvantaged. It has a reported graduation rate of 94% and yet the district fails to bring 90% of its male Black students from families eligible for the National Lunch Program to proficiency in grade 8 reading. Teachers and administrators in the Duval County school district decided to give one or more out-of-school suspensions to nearly three times the percentage of Black as to White students.

In the Hillsborough County district (Tampa), Newsome High School, which has a 2017 grade of "A" and an English Language Arts passing rate of 76%, is less than one-third minority and just 17% economically disadvantaged. It has a reported graduation rate of 98%. Chamberlain High School, which has a 2017 grade of "D" and an English Language Arts Achievement passing rate of 27%, is 82% minority (44% of whom are Hispanic and 28% Black) and 82% economically disadvantaged. It has a graduation rate of 72% and yet the district fails to bring 97% of its male Black students from families eligible for the National Lunch Program to proficiency in grade 8 reading. Teachers and administrators in the Hillsborough County school district decided to give one or more out-of-school suspension to three times the percentage of Black as White students (and more than twice the percentage of Hispanic students).

Conclusion

Black adult educational attainment in Florida is lower than the low national average. Why is that? A state's spending on education in relation to personal income is a measure of its commitment to education, or lack of commitment to education. Florida ranks as 50th among the states by this measure. In absolute terms, Florida spends just $8,900 per year per pupil on elementary and secondary education, ranking 44th among the states in support for education and well below both the national average of $11,400 and those of the neighboring states of Georgia and Alabama.[34] The difference from the national average would pay for at least one additional teacher per classroom. While Florida receives an average amount of per pupil revenue from Federal sources, and local sources provide only a slightly below average amount, the support of education from state revenue ($3,900) ranks only above Arizona and South Dakota—a thousand dollars per pupil less than Georgia and almost two thousand less than Alabama. This pin-points the responsibility for the lack of support for public education, and the lack of educational opportunities for Black students, in the state government: the governor and legislature.

This lack of commitment to public education is particularly damaging for the descendants of enslaved Africans living in Florida, with its history of discrimination—and worse—and its extraordinary underfunding of segregated schools before the 1950s as well as the large number of Black residents of the state who are recent immigrants from non-English-speaking Caribbean nations. The state's northern counties, such as Duval, differ little from neighboring fellow formerly Confederate areas in their treatment of Black students, while counties like Hillsborough continue to practice more or less explicit discriminatory segregation in their schools. (Hillsborough's neighboring Pinellas County has been cited for "re-segregating" its schools.) Florida could provide good educations for its Black children. It, and in particular the governor and state legislature, choose not to.

Three-Fifths of an Education

Texas

Florida, Texas and California each have large Black populations and larger Hispanic populations.

Texas, a former slave state and member of the Confederacy, has a slightly below average percentage of African-American residents (12%), but one of the largest Black populations in terms of absolute numbers (3.3 million). However, African-Americans are not the state's largest minority: approximately ten million of residents of the state are Hispanic, about one-third of whom are first-generation immigrants. The Black population of the state is concentrated in the Houston metropolitan area and along the border with Louisiana. The Hispanic population is concentrated along the border with Mexico, in some counties exceeding 90% of the population. The median family income of White, non-Hispanic, Texans is nearly double that that of Black and Hispanic families in the state (which are similar to one another), and White, non-Hispanic, poverty rates are approximately a third of the nearly identical Hispanic and Black poverty rates. Despite the fact that the combined Black and Hispanic population of Texas is only slightly greater than the White, non-Hispanic population, more than four times as many Black and Hispanic than White, non-Hispanic, people in Texas live in poverty. Or, to put that another way, poor people in Texas are most likely to be either Black or Hispanic.

More than one-third of Hispanic adults in Texas are without high school diplomas, compared to 17% of White, non-Hispanics, and just 11% of African-American adults. But 29% of White, non-Hispanic, adults have Bachelor's degrees or higher, compared to 21% of Black adults and only 14% of Hispanic adult Texans. One-third of Hispanics in the state are foreign-born and almost a third speak

135

English "less than very well." The African-American unemployment rate is 9%, the Hispanic unemployment rate is 6%, the White, non-Hispanic, unemployment rate is 5%. The median household income is $60,000 for White, non-Hispanics, $43,000 for African-American households and $45,000 for Hispanics.

White, non-Hispanics, in Texas are more highly educated, have lower unemployment and poverty rates and higher incomes than either Black or Hispanic residents of the state. It is an inequitable society divided along class and ethnic lines, as has been the case for more than two hundred years.

Prekindergarten and Its Effects

Prekindergarten classes have the potential for setting students on the path toward success in school, especially for the early primary grades. Texas enrolls approximately half of its 4-year-olds—including most Black and Hispanic 4-year olds—in the state-funded prekindergarten program. Nonetheless, while at grade four half of White, non-Hispanic, students read at grade level, which is above the national average for that group, just 17% of Black students and 22% of Hispanic fourth grade students read at grade level, despite the state's special provision of free prekindergarten for low income families. Part of the reason for these disappointing results may be the quality of the prekindergarten programs. The National Institute for Early Education Research rates Texas tenth in the nation for access to prekindergarten, but only 26th for funding of the program and finds, crucially, that the state does not meet quality standards for class size, staff-child ratios, meals or monitoring. This has effect on the fourth grade math and reading data: of the three large Texas districts for which the National Assessment of Educational Progress has data—Austin, Dallas and Houston—all achieve higher than state and national averages at fourth grade for their White, non-Hispanic, students (Austin achieving an extraordinary 70% reading at or above grade level), but fail to do so for their Black and Hispanic students. Dallas, in particular, has low, and identical, proficiency rates for Black and Hispanic students: 13%.

Income inequality runs along racial lines in Texas's major cities as well as in the state in general. According to the Brown University index, in which a value of 60 or above is considered to be a very high degree of segregation, Austin's index in 2010 was 70 (up from 50 in 1980) and 82% of Black students in the district were from lower-income families. The index for Dallas was 71 (with 93% of Black students from lower-income families), and Houston's index was 74, with 49% of Black students from lower-income families.

None of these districts have sufficient numbers of White students *eligible* for the National Lunch Program (that is, from lower-income families) for whom NAEP can report test results, and none have sufficient numbers of Black students *ineligible,* that is, middle class, for whom NAEP can report test results. The gap between how well White, non-Hispanic, students and Black students are taught reading in these districts is particularly stark. While a remarkable three-quarters of Austin's White, non-Hispanic, overwhelmingly middle-class students are taught to read at the level expected of them in fourth grade, the results for Black students did not meet NAEP's reporting standards, that is, in effect, the number of middle class Black students in Austin rounds to zero. In Dallas just 12% of Black students, all from lower-income families, reached grade level in reading, while the results for White, non-Hispanic, students did not meet NAEP's reporting standards: there were too few. And in Houston, as in Austin, three-quarters of the district's White, non-Hispanic, students from middle class families were taught to read at the level expected of fourth-graders, but in Houston, only 15% of the district's Black students from lower-income families had the opportunity to reach that level.

In sum, focusing on African-American residents of Texas, despite its state-wide prekindergarten program, Texas schools do not do well for their Black primary school students from poorer families—more than 80% of whom are not brought to grade level in reading in fourth grade.

Eighth Grade Reading
NAEP's state-wide results in grade eight reading for Texas show that 43% of White students reach or exceed proficiency (grade level), which is approximately the national average for that group, while

137

less than half that percentage, 19%, of Black and Hispanic students are taught to read by their schools at the level expected. The three NAEP-reported cities show disparate results. Austin and Houston are above the national average for White students (Austin at 65%), but all three are below both the state and national averages for Black and Hispanic students, averaging 89% of Black students and 84% of Hispanic students testing below grade level in reading. It is quite remarkable that Austin, that progressive city, can bring six times the percentage of its White, non-Hispanic, as it can, or will, its Black students to grade level in middle school.

The unusually high percentage of Black students reading at or above grade level in eighth grade in Texas (19%, compared to a national rate of 15%) can be traced to those among that state's comparatively few Black students whose families are sufficiently prosperous to make them ineligible for the National Lunch Program. Thirty-four percent of these students are brought to grade level. A Black student from one of these comparatively prosperous families in Texas is more likely to read at or above grade level at eighth grade than a White, non-Hispanic, student eligible for the National Lunch Program in the state. However, that economically disadvantaged White student is twice or more as likely to read at grade level in eighth grade as a Black student from a similarly impoverished background.

Parental education levels also play a part in student reading achievement. In Texas, a Black or White, non-Hispanic, student in eighth grade whose parents are college graduates has double the chance of reading proficiently as a student whose parents' education level is just that of high school graduation. Nonetheless, the percentage of White, non-Hispanic, students reading proficiently at grade eight whose parent has only a high school diploma is virtually the same as that of Black students whose parent graduated from college. Race matters in Texas even more than the cultural capital brought with increasing parental education.

None of the three districts with NAEP data have sufficient numbers of White students eligible for the National Lunch Program for whom to report test results for grade eight. For Black students, all three cities report that they fail to bring 91% of Black students from lower-income families to grade level. Only Houston has sufficient numbers of middle class Black students to report, bringing 23% to grade level in eighth grade.

Graduation Rates

The 4-year adjusted cohort graduation rate reported by Texas for the 2014-15 school year was 85% for Black students and 93% for White students. Part of that disparity may result from inequities in school discipline practices. In school year 2011-12, 13% of Black students in Texas and slightly less than a quarter of that percentage, 3%, of White students were given at least one out-of-school suspension. These exclusions from education are known to contribute to repeated grades and failure to graduate from high school.

Texas appears to be graduating few students with adequate reading skills. Only 15% of Black students and 42% of White students were reading at grade level in 2011, when they were in eighth grade. If we assume that all students reading at grade level in eighth grade graduated, it appears that just 16% of Black students in Texas and not even half of graduating White students were able to read at grade level when they received their diplomas. According to the College Board, only 13% of African-American SAT takers met the SAT College and Career Readiness Benchmark (as did 18% of Hispanic SAT takers). If Black graduation rates and percentages proficient at graduation in Texas were equal to current White outcomes, each year there would be an additional 16,700 college- and career-ready Black high school graduates in Texas (up from the estimated current 6,300).

Three-Fifths of an Education

Focus: Dallas and Houston

Dallas has a minority African-American population of 308,800 (24%).[35] Houston has 512,000 African-American residents (23%).[36] The cities' White residents are more highly educated, and their Black residents, less well educated than the national averages, with the anomaly for both that much higher percentages of the White population than the Black population, and much higher than national averages, are without high school diplomas. Family incomes for both Black and White residents of Dallas and Houston are below national averages and poverty rates higher.

Place	BA and Higher	No HS Diploma	Family Income	Unemployed	Poverty Rate
Black					
Dallas	17%	16%	$34,700	8%	30%
Houston	21%	11%	$37,800	10%	26%
U.S.	20%	15%	$45,000	11%	25%
White					
Dallas	38%	27%	$59,300	4%	19%
Houston	35%	24%	$60,700	5%	20%
U.S.	32%	11%	$73,000	5%	12%

The National Assessment of Educational Progress results for eighth grade reading for Dallas show that 10% of Black students are proficient and above (compared to 15% nationally). There were not sufficient numbers of White students in Dallas schools to meet NAEP reporting standards. Houston's public schools educate more than four times the percentage of their White students as their Black students to read at grade level in the crucial eighth grade year: 52% of White students are proficient and above (compared to 42% nationally) as are just 12% of Black students. 46% of Black students in the Houston public schools and 13% of White students were functionally illiterate, tested at the Below Basic level in 2015.

NAEP 2015 Eighth Grade Reading: Proficient and Above		
Place	**Black**	**White**
Dallas	10%	--
Houston	12%	52%
United States	15%	42%

Among Black students in Dallas, 9% of those eligible for the National Lunch Program read at or above the proficient level. Half, 49%, of Black students in the city's public schools were at the Below Basic level in 2015. Student educational attainment in Houston is also divided by income. White students in Houston from middle class families read at grade level 60% of the time in eighth grade. Among Black students, 9% of those eligible for the National Lunch Program read at or above the proficient level, while more than twice as many, 23%, of those from more prosperous Black families do so. A White, non-Hispanic, student from a comparatively prosperous family in Houston is nearly seven times as likely to be brought to grade level in eighth grade reading than a Black student from a low-income family in either city.

In school year 2013-14, 18% of Black students in Dallas and 6% of White students were given at least one out-of-school suspension.[37] Thirteen percent of Black students in Houston and 4% of White students were given at least one out-of-school suspension.[38] Teachers and local school administrators in Dallas and Houston are three times as likely to exclude Black students from the classroom as they are to exclude White, non-Hispanic, students.

The 4-year adjusted cohort graduation rate reported by Dallas for the 2015-16 school year was 85% for Black students and 92% for White students (national rates were 74.6% for Black students and 87.6% for White students).[39] Given that only 9% of Black students and 46% of White students were reading at grade level in 2011, when they were in eighth grade, and that nationally, there is only a small (one or two point) difference between eighth grade and twelfth grade achievement levels in reading, it appears that 74-76% of graduating Black students in Dallas and about half of graduating White students received their diplomas while having serious deficiencies in their reading skills. The 4-year adjusted cohort graduation rate reported by Houston for the 2015-16 school year was 84% for Black students and 91% for White students.[40] Given that only 11% of Black students and 56% of White students were reading at grade level in 2011, when they were in eighth grade, it appears that 71-73% of graduating Black students in Houston and about a third of graduating White students received their diplomas while having serious deficiencies in their reading skills.

Conclusion: Texas

The Public Policy Research Center study of school discipline practice ("Breaking School Rules") found that in Texas school employee responses to student actions leading to suspension and the like varied with race and ethnicity. White, non-Hispanic, students were treated most leniently, Hispanic students more severely, and Black students the most severely of all. It is not impossible that the differences in the way that African-American students are treated by Texas school employees in the behavioral context is also the case for how they are treated in the academic context, resulting in the dire academic achievement documented above.

As we have seen, White, non-Hispanic, educational attainment in Texas, as measured by the percentage of adults with a Bachelor's degree or greater, is nearly twice that of Black adults in the state. White, non-Hispanic, median family income is nearly twice that of mean Black family income. The percentage of White, non-Hispanic, students in eighth grade who are taught well enough to read proficiently is more than twice that of Black students. These matters are connected: grade eight reading proficiency plays an important, if not determining, role in preparation for high school graduation, college and careers.

Texas ranks 43rd in overall per pupil elementary and secondary school system spending and 47th in the amount of that from the state. It ranks 31st in per pupil expenditure in relation to personal income, a measure of effort, or commitment to education. As with prekindergarten finance, Texas schools are not as good as they might be for Black students (and more generally, for students from lower-income families), because the state is unwilling to pay for them. This is the direct responsibility of the governor and state legislature. If they wanted better schools for the state's most vulnerable students, they would pay for them. They do not pay for them.

Three-Fifths of an Education

California

Like Florida and Texas, California has a large Black population and a larger Hispanic population.

California has a comparatively low percentage of African-American residents (7%), just over half the national average, but, as a destination for mid-twentieth-century Black migration, it has one of the larger Black populations in terms of absolute numbers (2.3 million). Like those of Texas and Florida, California's population of African-American residents is outnumbered by Hispanic residents, about one-third of whom are first-generation immigrants.[41] African-American Californians are less likely to have dropped out-of-school than the national average for the group (as well as the average for White, non-Hispanic, Californians) and considerably more likely to have graduated from college than Black residents of other states. The gap in academic attainment between Black and White, non-Hispanics, is narrower in California than nationally. Similarly, median Black family incomes in the state are much higher than the national average for Black families and the income, unemployment and poverty rate gaps are narrower. California's African-American workers are more likely to be employed in management, business, science and arts occupations than the national average for the group and less likely to be employed in service occupations. Nonetheless, Black Californians are much less likely to have graduated from college than White, non-Hispanic, Californians, are more likely to be unemployed, have just two-thirds the average family income and are much more likely to live in poverty. Much of these differences can be attributed to the shortcomings of the state's education system.

California enrolls 35% of its 4-year-old children in the state's prekindergarten programs according to the National Institute for

Three-Fifths of an Education

Early Education Research, which should have positive effects on learning in the primary grades. Nonetheless, in fourth grade, while White, non-Hispanic, students are taught to read at national averages for the group, Black (and Hispanic) students are taught less well than their peers nationally. More than half of Black fourth-graders test at the Below Basic level," essentially unable to read and almost 90% are below grade level. That situation is nearly reversed for White, non-Hispanic, students, nearly half of whom are brought to grade level in reading in fourth grade.

California schools educate their Black and White, non-Hispanic, middle school students to slightly above the national average levels of achievement, but nonetheless educate just over a third as many of their Black students as their White students to read at grade level in the crucial eighth grade year. Over 80% of California's Black students have not been taught to read at grade level in eighth grade. While just 15% of the state's White, non-Hispanic, students are left functionally illiterate in middle school, 40% of the state's Black students test at that Below Basic level. California has particularly large income-based gaps within both its Black and White students, with twice the percentage of each from relatively prosperous families reading at grade level than those eligible for the National Lunch Program.

A White student from California from a lower-income family, and therefore qualifying for the National Lunch Program, is twice or more as likely to read at grade level in eighth grade as a Black student from a similarly impoverished background, and slightly more likely to read at grade level than a Black student from a middle class family. White students from middle class families are more than twice as likely to read at grade level as are Black students who are similarly ineligible for the National Lunch Program and four times as likely as Black students eligible for the National Lunch Program.

Among the state's large school districts, San Diego's school system is particularly successful in minimizing the percentage of students at the Below Basic level for both Black and White students. And then there is Fresno. This city in the agricultural center of California does little to educate any of its children. Even among White, non-Hispanic, students, 36% are functionally illiterate in

146

middle school, compared to a national average for the group of 16%. And most, 55%, of Black eighth graders in the city's schools test at that Below Basic level. Just 8% of Black eighth graders in Fresno are assessed by NAEP to read at grade level, slightly over half of the low national average for that group.

Residential, and consequent school, segregation may contribute to the fact that while the percentage of eighth grade White, non-Hispanic, students in the state reaching proficiency increases with each increment of parental education, approximately following the national pattern for that group, the percentage of Black students in eighth grade reading at grade level shows no improvement at all between those whose parents had just some education after high school and those who are the children of college graduates. Perhaps they all go to the same under-resourced schools, as residential patterns in California, and therefore its school systems, are severely segregated. In the Los Angeles metropolitan area the White/Black Index of Dissimilarity from Brown University has a reading of 65 (a value of 60 is considered very high). In the San Francisco metropolitan area, the White-Black Index of Dissimilarity is 59. The Indices of Dissimilarity for both Black and Hispanic students in the Los Angeles Unified School District are 75 and 77, respectively. The average Black student in L.A. is in a school that is 60% poor, the average Hispanic student is in a school that is 66% poor, but the average White, non-Hispanic, student is in a school that is just 36% poor. These figures are similar in San Diego, slightly less severe in San Francisco.

In the 2011-12 school year, 15% of Black students in California and a third of that percentage, 5%, of White, non-Hispanic, students were given at least one out-of-school suspension by school officials. Research has shown that disparities of this type can be attributed to the racial prejudices of school officials and that they contribute to the likelihood of Black students not reaching high school graduation.

147

Three-Fifths of an Education

Focus: Los Angeles

Los Angeles has a below average minority African-American population (9%) of 364,700.[42] Both Black and White, non-Hispanic, Los Angeles adults are more likely to have advanced educations than the national average. Family incomes in Los Angeles are about average for each group. Los Angeles's public schools educate between two and three times the percentage of their White students as their Black students to read at grade level in the crucial eighth grade year. Nearly half, 42%, of Black students in the city's public schools and 17% of White students were functionally illiterate, tested at the Below Basic level in 2015.

Student educational attainment in Los Angeles is sharply divided by income as well as by race. Just 11% of students from lower-income Black families read at grade level in middle school, compared to half, 54%, of White, non-Hispanic, students from middle class families. There are too few White students from families living in or near poverty, and therefore eligible for the National Lunch Program, and too few Black families, ineligible, in the Los Angeles public schools to meet NAEP's reporting standards. However, NAEP does find that a White student from a comparatively prosperous family in Los Angeles is nearly five times as likely to be brought to grade level in eighth grade reading than a Black student from a low-income family.

The most recent year for which district-level school discipline data is available from the U.S. Department of Education's Office for Civil Rights is 2013-14. That year, 3% of Black students in Los Angeles and 1% of White students were given at least one out-of-school suspension.[43] Or, to put that another way, school level administrators and teachers in Los Angeles are three times as likely to remove Black students from the classroom as they are to inflict that punishment on White, non-Hispanic, students.

The 4-year adjusted cohort graduation rate reported by Los Angeles for the 2015-16 school year was 67% for Black students and 91% for White students (national rates were 74.6% for Black students and 76% for White students).[44] Given that only 15% of Black students and 41% of White students were reading at grade level in 2011, when they were in eighth grade, and that nationally, there is only a small (one or two point) difference between eighth grade and twelfth grade achievement levels in reading, it appears that 50-52% of graduating Black students in Los Angeles and about a third of graduating White students received their diplomas while having serious deficiencies in their reading skills.

Graduation Rates: California

The 4-year adjusted cohort graduation rate reported by California as a whole for the 2014-15 school year was 71% for Black students and 88% for White students (national rates were 74.6% for Black students and 87.6% for White students).[45] As only 16% of California's Black students and 44% of White students were reading at grade level in 2011, when they were in eighth grade, it appears that just 14% of Black students in California graduated being able to read at the level expected of eighth graders, as did 38%, of White students.

California's Hispanic and Black Educational Achievement

California has nearly six million White, non-Hispanic, students, five million Hispanic students and approximately 600,000 Black students. At grade eight, 18% of Hispanic students in California read at grade level or above, as do 16% of Black students and 44% of non-Hispanic White students. The percentage of White, non-Hispanic, students reading at or above grade level is more than two and a half times that for Hispanic students and there is the same gap for Black students.

We can examine the differences between Black, White and Hispanic educational achievement by looking at language issues. NAEP disaggregates data by whether a student speaks a language other than English in the home, an indicator of assimilation. In California, Hispanic students who never speak a language other than English at home reach the proficient or above level in grade eight reading five percentage points more often than Black students. At the other end of the linguistic spectrum, in California, Hispanic students who speak Spanish at home all or most of the time reach grade level in eighth grade reading at the same rate as Black students who never speak a language other than English. In no case, at any amount of Hispanic English language usage, does California educate its Black students to a higher level of achievement than its Hispanic students. There is little variation between the achievement levels in grade eight reading for Hispanic students who always speak (presumably) Spanish at home and those who never do so in California or nationally. On the other hand, parental education is a strong variable, with the percentage of Hispanic students reading at grade level in middle school doubling between those with parents who did not finish high school and those whose parents graduated from college.

Conclusion

In California 21% of African-American SAT takers met the 2015 SAT College and Career Readiness Benchmark (as compared to 16% nationally for African-Americans and 53% for White SAT takers). We can assume that only those students intended to go to college are "SAT takers." While about half of White, non-Hispanic, Californian 18- to 24-year-olds were enrolled in degree-granting postsecondary institutions in 2015, just 39% of Black 18- to 24-year-olds were, which was slightly better than the national average (as were enrollment percentages for all groups), but one more indication of the inferiority of their educational opportunities in the state.[46] If Black graduation rates and percentages proficient at graduation in California were equal to current White outcomes, each year there would be an additional 11,500 college- and career-ready Black high school graduates in California (up from the estimated current 2,300).

There are large gaps between White, non-Hispanic, and Black achievement at every educational level in the state. Although Black adult educational attainment in California is considerably higher than the national average and Black family incomes are considerably higher in California than the national average, both lag those measures for White, non-Hispanics. California spends less per pupil than the national average, ranking 31st in the country and less than half of that of New York State, for example, and is 39th in the relation between school spending and personal income, a measure of effort.[47] The state could, and should, do much better.

Tennessee

Tennessee and Maryland are former slave states that did not join the Confederacy.

There are an equal percentage of descendents of enslaved Africans in Tennessee who are without a high school diploma as the percentage who have graduated from college, while there are twice as many White, non-Hispanic, residents of the state who have graduated from college as the percentage that are without high school diplomas. With an above average percentage of African-American residents (17%), and one of the larger Black populations in terms of absolute numbers (1,200,00), Tennessee maintains twice the percentage of African-Americans in poverty as the White population, nearly twice the percentage of unemployed adults and Black family incomes only two-thirds as great as White family incomes. This imbalance in educational attainment and incomes is traceable to the inequitable opportunities for education offered by the state's schools.

Tennessee has great economic disparities within its racial groups. The Appalachian counties on the eastern border of the state are all over 90% White, with median household incomes in the $30-49,000 range, while incomes in the counties in the center of the state, equally White, are $80,000 and higher. But the economic disparities between the races are even greater. The African-American population of the state is concentrated in its southeastern corner, where Memphis is the economic center of the Mississippi Delta region. State-wide, the percentage of Black families with incomes under $10,000 per year, 13%, is almost three times that of White families living in such extreme poverty (although the *number* of White families in that category is double that of Black families). Approximately equal percentages of White families have incomes under $10,000 per year and over $200,000. The more compressed, and lower, income distribution of Black families is illustrated by the fact that the percentage of African-American families in the state with incomes over $200,000 is just 1%. Only if we add together all Black families with incomes of $80,000 and greater can we match the percentage of Black families with incomes under $10,000 per year.

Tennessee's schools leave twice the percentage of Black as White, non-Hispanic, students at the Below Basic level on the National Assessment of Educational Progress test in reading in fourth grade (55% to 27%) and helps less than half as many read at grade level (17% to 40%). Among students from lower-income families (those eligible for the National Lunch Program), half again as many Black as White students are at the functionally illiterate Below Basic level (59% to 38%) and only a little more than half the percentage of Black as White students are brought to grade level in reading (14% to 25%). Among middle class students in primary school, the proportions are similarly inequitable, with more than twice the percentage of Black students from families with incomes making them ineligible for the national lunch program as White students from middle class families being left at the Below Basic level ((36% to 16%) and less than half as many reaching the proficient or above levels (25% to 53%).

By eighth grade, results on the NAEP for Tennessee schools are slightly lower than national averages for both White, non-Hispanic, and Black students. More than twice the percentage of White as Black students have been taught to read at grade level (15% to 38%) and more than twice the percentage of Black as White remain functionally illiterate (44% to 18%). The same holds for the distributions within income categories. White students from families in Tennessee living in or near poverty, and therefore eligible for the National Lunch Program, read at grade level at eighth grade 24% of the time, while other White students, from more prosperous families, read at grade level more than twice as often: 49% of the time in eighth grade. Among Black students, just 10% of those eligible for the National Lunch Program read at or above the proficient level, while almost three times as many, 29%, of those from more prosperous families do so, a larger percentage than that of National Lunch Program eligible White students. Here, again, the state enables approximately equal percentages of middle class Black students and lower-income White students to read at grade level, but a White student from a comparatively prosperous family in Tennessee is nearly five times as likely to be brought to grade level in eighth grade reading as a Black student from a low-income family.

NAEP has found that virtually no Black eighth grade students whose parents did not finish high school were brought to grade level reading by their schools in Tennessee (as compared to 16% of the White children of parents without diplomas). A White child of high school graduates is more likely to read proficiently in middle school than a Black child of college graduates (23% to 21%). Students in the state's suburban schools are much more likely to read proficiently in eighth grade than students in urban or rural school (44% to 29% and 31%), but as NAEP did not find a sufficient number of Black students attending suburban schools in Tennessee to report their achievement level, the suburban school educational advantage in the state accrues almost entirely to White students. Among city school students, nearly half (46%) of White students read at grade level, just under four times the percentage of their Black peers (12%). In Tennessee's rural schools, a third of White students are taught to read proficiently, but only 13% of rural Black students have that opportunity.

There is no NAEP data for individual cities in Tennessee and there are complications with the state testing program. Be that as it may, the economic and racial disparities in the state can be explored by comparing the Shelby County schools to the Nashville-Davidson schools, a relatively high income area in the state's center. About 20% of Black adults in Memphis lack a high school diploma and about 14% are college graduates. Comparable White, non-Hispanic, figures are 8% without a diploma and 42% college graduates. Median Black household income is $33,300 and median White household income is $54,000. The Shelby County schools, which include Memphis, have an enrollment of 112,000, 60% of whom are "economically disadvantages (by state standards) and 78% of whom are Black. The graduation rate is reported as 79%; the percentage of students who meet the composite score on the ACT, qualifying them for the HOPE Scholarship is 21.6%. In comparison, about 15% of Black adults in Nashville lack a high school diploma and about 23% are college graduates. Comparable White, non-Hispanic, figures are 10% without a diploma and 33% college graduates. Median Black family income is $36,000 and median White household income is $57,000. The Davidson County public schools, including Nashville, enroll 85,000 students, of whom 54% are economically disadvantaged and 44% of whom are Black. The graduation rate is reported as 81%, the percentage of students who meet the composite score on the ACT, qualifying them for the HOPE Scholarship is 31.3%. In other words, in the White majority Nashville schools a student has half again as great a chance of becoming college ready as a student in the Black majority Memphis schools.

Returning to the state overview, in school year 2013-14, 20% of Black students in Tennessee and just 4% of White students were given at least one out-of-school suspension. That five-fold difference is arguably a measure of racial prejudice among Tennessee's teachers and school-level administrators.

Tennessee is 45th in per pupil spending and also 45th in relation to school system finance amounts to $1,000 personal income. In other words, it could invest more in education, but chooses not to. The result is that although the 4-year adjusted cohort graduation rate reported by Tennessee for the 2014-15 school year was 81% for Black students and 91% for White students, given that only 15% of Black students and 38% of White students were reading at grade level in 2011, it appears that 90% of graduating Black students in Tennessee and almost two-thirds of graduating White students received their diplomas while having serious deficiencies in their reading skills. This is confirmed by an ACT finding that just 20% of ACT-tested Tennessee high school graduates met all ACT College Readiness Benchmarks in 2016 and that just 9% of African-American graduates met three or more of the benchmarks (while 38% of White graduates did so). If Black students graduated career- and college-ready at the same rate as White, non-Hispanic students, the state would benefit by the addition of 5,000 more well-educated Black students each year than the current 1,300.

Why does it not? This is the result of decisions by the governor and state legislature, by the state and district education authorities, by state and local administrators. The relationship between the state government and the schools in the Memphis area, with its large, impoverished, Black population, is troubled. Support for schools there, and elsewhere in the state, by Tennessee's governmental officials has been insufficient. The limited educational opportunities of the descendents of enslaved Africans in Tennessee are their personal responsibilities.

Three-Fifths of an Education

Maryland

Maryland, a former slave state that did not join the Confederacy, has a high percentage of African-American residents (30%), and one of the larger Black populations: 1.8 million. Median Black and median White, non-Hispanic, family incomes in Maryland are much higher than national averages and the poverty rates in Maryland are very much lower than the national average for each group. Considerably higher than average percentages of both Black and White residents of Maryland have Bachelor's degrees or higher qualifications. However, as we have come to expect, to think it almost natural, Maryland's Black incomes and educational attainment are lower than that of White residents of the state and the Black poverty rate in Maryland is more than twice as high as that of White Maryland residents.

The state's Black population is concentrated in three counties and one city: Somerset County, in the extreme southern part of the Eastern Shore of the state, Charles and Prince George's counties in the southwest, and Baltimore City. As with other states that extend into the Appalachian region, Maryland's lowest median family incomes are in its two far western Appalachian counties, which are almost completely White, as well as in Somerset County and Baltimore, with their concentrations of Black residents. Charles and Prince George's counties have very high median family incomes, considering their predominance of Black families. The wealth of the state and the comparative prosperity and educational attainment of its Black residents are in large part artifacts of federal employment in Washington, D.C. and its suburbs.

Three-Fifths of an Education

Educational Achievement

More than a third, 36%, of Maryland's four-year-olds are enrolled in preschool. The state ranks 13th in access to preschool, but only 33rd in spending for preschool programs, meaning that it could do even better, if its governor and state legislature so decided. Half (48%) of students from lower-income families test at Below Basic, that is, functionally illiterate, on the National Assessment of Educational Progress tests in fourth grade, compared with just 18% of students from middle class families. More than half (53%) of students from middle class families are assessed at grade level, compared to just 18% of students from lower-income families. Those results by income might just as well serve as a proxy for results by race, as 48% of Black students and just 19% of White students are assessed as functionally illiterate and 51% of White fourth-grade students read proficiently, compared to just 18% of Black students. Among students from middle class Black families, 27% read proficiently in primary school, while more than twice that percentage, 58%, of middle class White students are taught to do so. These results are at, or slightly below, national averages.

Middle school reading ability of students in Maryland is much better than national averages. Nonetheless, the racial gap remains. The percentage of Black students reading at grade level or above in grade 8 in Maryland is 19%, compared to the national average of 14%. Among White students it is 50%, compared to the national average of 42%. Forty percent of Maryland's Black students test as functionally illiterate in eighth grade, compared to just 13% of White students.

Student educational attainment in Maryland, as elsewhere, is sharply divided by income differences within races. Only a quarter of White students from lower-income families in Maryland read at grade level in eighth grade, while twice that proportion, half of other White students, those from more prosperous families, read at or above grade level. Among Maryland's Black students (as nationally) just 12% of those eligible for the National Lunch Program score at or above proficient in reading, while, again, more than twice as many, 29%, of those from more prosperous families do so.

By the admittedly low national standards Maryland is remarkably successful in educating its Black children whose family incomes are sufficient to make them ineligible for the National Lunch Program. A Black student from a comparatively prosperous family in Maryland is more likely to read at or above grade level at eighth grade than a White student eligible for the National Lunch Program in the state and nearly twice as likely to read at or above grade level as the average Black student, nationally. And yet students from middle class Black families in Maryland are far behind their White economic peers in the state. Excellent suburban schools can do only so much to overcome centuries of disadvantage and to level a playing field tilted by an income distribution drastically favoring White families, and can do nothing for Black students attending inferior urban schools. As a result, the combined racial and economic gap in Maryland is dramatic. A White student from a comparatively prosperous family in Maryland is nearly five times as likely to be brought to grade level in eighth grade reading as a Black student from a low-income family in the state.

School Discipline
School discipline data highlights the differences in the ways that Black children are treated in Maryland. In 2011-12, 9% of Black students (and 12% of male Black students) in Maryland were given at least one out-of-school suspension, while less than half that percentage, 4%, of White students (and 12% of male White students) were. Maryland school officials were more than twice as likely to restrict access to classrooms for Black students as for White students.[48] Out-of-school suspensions efficiently increase the likelihood that students will be required to repeat a grade and then drop out-of-school entirely.

High School Graduation Rates and Validity
In Maryland, the 4-year adjusted cohort graduation rate for Black students in the 2014-15 school year was 82%; for White students Maryland reported 92%.[49] 19% of Black students and 50% of White students were reading at grade level in 2011, when they were in

Three-Fifths of an Education

eighth grade. It then appears that just 17% of Black students in Maryland and half of White students received their diplomas with reading skills at the grade 8 level or above. Just 16% of Maryland's African-American SAT takers met the SAT College and Career Readiness Benchmark. If the state of Maryland educated its students who are the descendents of enslaved Africans as well as it educates its White, non-Hispanic students, 19,800 rather than just 3,200 would each year graduate college- and career-ready.

Focus: Baltimore City and the District of Columbia

Although the city of Washington is not part of the state of Maryland, it is intimately connected to the state's economy and culture. Both Washington, D.C. and Baltimore are historically, culturally, southern cities. Baltimore has a majority African-American population of 394,000.[50] Washington has slightly smaller African-American population, 311,000.[51] Baltimore's Black population has a much lower level of educational attainment than the national average, a lower median family income, and higher unemployment rate. Washington has an average level of Black educational attainment and income and a higher than average unemployment rate. In contrast, the District's White population has very high levels of educational attainment and income, and very low levels of unemployment and poverty.

Place	BA and Higher	No HS Diploma	Family Income	Unemployed	Poverty Rate
Black					
Baltimore	5%	25%	$40,000	15%	20%
Washington	22%	19%	$46,000	17%	22%
U.S.	20%	15%	$45,000	11%	25%
White					
Baltimore	23%	18%	$72,400	6%	8%
Washington	82%	5%	$160,400	3%	3%
U.S.	32%	11%	$73,000	5%	12%

The National Assessment of Educational Progress results for eighth grade reading for Baltimore show that 36% of White students are proficient and above (compared to 42% nationally) as are just 10% of Black students (compared to 15% nationally). More than half of Black students in the city's public schools and a quarter of White students were at the Below Basic level in 2015: they were

161

Three-Fifths of an Education

functionally illiterate. Baltimore's public schools educate between three and four times the percentage of their White students as they do their Black students to read at grade level in middle school, while Washington's public schools educate more than seven times the percentage of their White students as their Black students to read at grade level in the crucial eighth grade year. NAEP results for eighth grade reading for Washington show that 75% of White students are proficient and above as are just 10% of Black students. 56% of Black students in the city's public schools and 5% of White students were at the Below Basic level in 2015. It would be hard to argue otherwise than that the District of Columbia maintains separate schools systems for Black and White students.

NAEP 2015 Eighth Grade Reading: Proficient and Above		
District	Black	White
Baltimore	10%	36%
Washington	10%	75%

There are too few White students in the Baltimore public schools for NAEP to report White assessments by income. Among Black students, 8% of those eligible for the National Lunch Program read at or above the proficient level, while 14%, of those from more prosperous families do so. A White student (at any income level) in Baltimore is more than four as likely to be brought to grade level in eighth grade reading than a Black student from a low-income family. Student educational attainment in Washington is also sharply divided by income. There are too few White students from families living in or near poverty, and therefore eligible for the National Lunch Program, in the Washington public schools for NAEP to report their assessments. Other White students, from more prosperous families, read at grade level 78% of the time in eighth grade. Among Black students, 7% of those eligible for the National Lunch Program read at or above the proficient level, while nearly five times as many, 33%, of those from more prosperous families do so.

NAEP 2015 Eighth Grade Reading: Proficient and Above				
	Black		White	
District	NLP Eligible	NLP Ineligible	NLP Eligible	NLP Ineligible
Baltimore	8%	14%	--	--
Washington	7%	33%	--	78%

A Black student from a comparatively prosperous family in Baltimore is much less likely to read at or above grade level at eighth grade than an average White student eligible for the National Lunch Program in the state of Maryland as a whole. A White student from a comparatively prosperous family in Washington is more than eleven times as likely to be brought to grade level in eighth grade reading than a Black student from a low-income family. A Black student from a comparatively prosperous family in Washington is more than twice as likely to read at or above grade level at eighth grade as the national average for Black students, and slightly above the rate for White students from Alabama, Louisiana and New York State.

In the 2013-14 school year, 7% of Black students in Baltimore and 3% of White students were given at least one out-of-school suspension.[52] Seventeen percent of Black students in Washington and 1% of White students were given at least one out-of-school suspension.[53] Baltimore teachers are twice as likely, and Washington, D.C., teachers are *seventeen times* as likely, to remove Black students from the classroom as they are to interrupt the education of White students.

The 4-year adjusted cohort graduation rate reported by Baltimore for the 2015-16 school year was 71% for Black students and 70% for White students (national rates were 74.6% for Black students and 87.6% for White students).[54] Given that only 8% of Black students and 34% of White students were reading at grade level in 2011, when they were in eighth grade, it appears that 61-63% of graduating Black students in Baltimore and about half of graduating White students received their diplomas while having serious deficiencies in their reading skills. The 4-year adjusted cohort graduation rate reported by the District of Columbia for the 2015-16 school year was

67% for Black students and 93% for White students.[55] Given that only 10% of Black students and 63% of White students were reading at grade level in 2011, it appears that 65-67% of graduating Black students in Washington and about a third of graduating White students received their diplomas while having serious deficiencies in their reading skills. Unusually, all Washington, D.C., students from the graduating class of 2015 took the SAT. Of those, just 12% of African-American SAT takers met the SAT College and Career Readiness benchmark.

Conclusion: Maryland

By most measures, Maryland's population is wealthier and more highly educated, with better educational achievement levels, than the national averages for both Black and White students. But there are broad racial and income inequities in the state. The percentage of White students from families with incomes eligible for the National Lunch Program (18%) is only just over half that of the percentage of middle income Black families (33%). Most Black families are in the lower-income quintiles; most White, non-Hispanic, families are in the middle and higher income quintiles. There is a thirty-point racial gap in the percentage of middle school students reading at grade level. Although Maryland ranks eleventh in per pupil funding of public schools it is 23rd in relation to school finance per $1,000 of personal income. In other words it could, and should, do better. The fact that it does not is the personal responsibility of the governor and members of the state legislature, state and local school boards and administrators.

Illinois

Illinois was among the most important industrial states of twentieth century and among the principal destinations of the Great Migration of the descendants of enslaved Africans from the Jim Crow former slave states of the south. It now has a comparatively average percentage of African-American residents (14%) with one of the larger Black populations in terms of absolute numbers (1.8 million). While more than a third of White, non-Hispanic, adults in the state have a college education, only one fifth of Black adults have reached that level of educational attainment. Fewer White, non-Hispanic, adults in the state have failed to achieve a high school diploma than the national average for that group, but a higher percentage of Black adults in Illinois than nationally have not graduated from high school. White family median income in Illinois is higher, and Black family median income is lower, than the national average for each group and Black families live on just over half of the incomes available to White families, with a poverty rate more than three times as great.

Race	BA and Higher	No HS Diploma	Family Income	Unemployed	Poverty Rate
Illinois					
Black	20%	14%	$42,500	10%	24%
White	35%	9%	$81,000	3%	7%
United States					
Black	20%	11%	$45,000	11%	25%
White	32%	15%	$73,000	5%	12%

Prekindergarten

High quality prekindergarten programs have positive effects that continue to be evident through the primary grades. Illinois enrolls 26% of its 4-year-olds and 20% of its 3-year-old children in the state's prekindergarten programs, a particularly high percentage for 3-year olds, giving it a national rank of third for access for those children.[56] The rank for access for 4-year-olds is 21st, according to the National Institute for Early Education Research. Illinois's prekindergarten meets almost all of NIEER's "quality standards." The state is, however, remiss in spending on prekindergarten, ranking 34th. In other words, Illinois runs a good prekindergarten program for the quarter or less of children for whom it provides funding.

White, non-Hispanic, fourth graders in Illinois reach proficiency at a rate identical to the national average for that group (46%), while Illinois' Black fourth graders are taught to read to grade level at a third of that rate and well beneath the national average for Black students in the fourth grade (15% compared to 18%). Primary school outcomes in Illinois for White, non-Hispanic, students are similar to national averages for those children both from lower-income and those from middle class families, while outcomes for Black children are much lower than the national average for Black children from lower-income families, while higher for those from middle class families (which, as a matter of fact, are higher than those of White, non-Hispanic, children from lower-income families). Nearly 90% of Black children in Illinois from lower-income families do not read proficiently in fourth grade, while nearly 60%, tested at the Below Basic level, have little, if any, of the reading skills required at that point in their educations.

Eighth Grade Reading

The National Assessment of Educational Progress results for eighth grade reading for Illinois show that 45% of White students are proficient and above (slightly above the percentage nationally) as are 13% of Black students (slightly below the percentage nationally). Illinois educates its White students, by this measure, three times as well as it educates its Black students. Nearly half, 44%, of Black students in the state are assessed as "Below Basic," that is, functionally illiterate, at grade eight, three times the rate for White, non-Hispanic, students.

As elsewhere, student educational attainment in Illinois is divided by income as well as by race. White students from families living in or near poverty, and therefore eligible for the National Lunch Program, read at grade level (proficient or above) at eighth grade just under two-thirds as often as those from more prosperous White families in Illinois. Black students from lower-income families read at grade level at eighth grade a third as often as students from more prosperous Black families in the state. The gap between Black students from lower-income families and White students from prosperous families is more than forty percentage points. The gap based on income among White students is approximately twenty points; among Black students it is seventeen points.

NAEP 2015 Eighth Grade Reading: Proficient and Above				
	Black		White	
Place	NLP Eligible	NLP Ineligible	NLP Eligible	NLP Ineligible
Illinois	10%	27%	32%	51%
US Public	12%	26%	27%	50%

A White student from a comparatively prosperous family in Illinois is approximately five times as likely to be brought to grade level in eighth grade reading than a Black student from a low-income family. A Black student from a comparatively prosperous family in Illinois is not as likely to read at or above grade level at eighth grade as a White student eligible for the National Lunch Program. The percentage of lower-income White, non-Hispanic, students reading at grade level in Illinois increases between fourth and eighth grade, that of lower-income Black students decreases with those additional years in the state's schools.

Out-of-School Suspensions
Out-of-school suspensions, an efficient way to discourage students from completing their educations, have been shown to more accurately reflect the racial attitudes of school-level personnel than variations in student behavior. In the 2011-12 school year, more than four times the percentage of Black students in Illinois (16%} as of White students (3.5%) were given at least one out-of-school suspension.

Graduation Rates
The 4-year adjusted cohort graduation rate reported by Illinois for the 2014-15 school year was 75.5% for Black students and 90% for White students (national rates were 74.6% for Black students and 87.6% for White students).[57] Given that only 13% of Black students and 45% of White students were reading at grade level in 2011, when they were in eighth grade, it appears that just 13% of Black students in Illinois and less than half (42%) of White students

received their diplomas while reading at grade 8 proficiency or better.

If we take reading proficiency as a rough measure, Illinois, which provides an above average amount of funding to education, educates its White students at a rate three times that of its Black students. It leaves a quarter of its Black students without high school diplomas and half of those who manage to stay in school until grade 12 functionally illiterate (tested as Below Basic by NAEP). Four-fifths of the Black students in Illinois, and just under a half of the White students, who graduate do so not having been taught to read at grade level in middle school. That is not a good record for White students. It is a catastrophe for Black students. It is particularly catastrophic for male Black students, more than half of whom are left functionally illiterate in eighth grade. It is not then surprising that a third of the state's male Black ninth grade students have left school by their senior year.

If Black graduation rates and percentages proficient at graduation were equal to current White outcomes, each year there would be an additional 10,000 college- and career-ready Black high school graduates in Illinois (up from the estimated current 2,400).

Three-Fifths of an Education

Much of this problem is concentrated in Chicago, with nearly half the state's Black population. Which brings us to the question: Are Chicago's public schools to be trusted with the education of the city's Black children? There is a short answer to that question, based on the district's record. That answer is "no."

The graduation rate reported by Chicago for the 2015-16 school year was 67% for Black students and 86% for White students. Given that only 13% of Black students and 41% of White students were reading at grade level in 2011, when they were in eighth grade, it appears that fewer than ten percent of Black students and about one-third of White, non-Hispanic, students entering high school in Chicago received their diplomas four years later without serious deficiencies in their reading skills.

Some observers point out that four years of college are not necessary for all students (although they rarely assert that a four-year college degree is not necessary for their own children). However, it is widely agreed that the types of certification and training provided by community colleges are increasingly essential. Being prepared for classes at a four-year or community college is, for all practical purposes, the equivalent of having graduated "college- and career-ready." A useful measure of the success (or lack of it) of Chicago's school system is whether its graduates are prepared at least for community college classes. Are they? They are not. Seventy percent of all Chicago students enrolling in community colleges take remedial courses, that is, the Chicago Public Schools fail to educate more than two-thirds of the students in its care to the standard expected for the type of career-preparation provided by community colleges. As a matter of fact, according to the Illinois Report Card, just 30% of all of Chicago's graduating seniors meet the ACT College Readiness Benchmark.

This situation is, of course, particularly dire for male Black students.

Of the male Black students in Chicago's ninth grade classrooms in 2012, less than 60% graduated four years later. Of those, about half, 31%, of the group that had been together in ninth grade enrolled in colleges, including community colleges. More than two-thirds

170

either did not get a high school diploma or having graduated did not go on to college. These proportions were reversed for the district's White, non-Hispanic, male students, nearly two-thirds of whom graduated from high school and then enrolled in college.

The failure of the Chicago Public Schools to educate Black children can be traced back through the grades to its failure to teach them the basic skill of reading. According to the National Assessment of Educational Progress, Chicago's public schools teach more than four times the percentage of their White students as that of their Black students to read at grade level in the crucial eighth grade year: 63% as compared to 13%. Nearly half, 44%, of all Black students in the city's middle schools, as compared to just 10% of White students, are at the Below Basic level, that is, functionally illiterate. And over 90% of male Black students are not taught to read at grade level in Chicago's middle schools. Of those most in need of help from their schools, African-American students whose parents had attained only a high school diploma, just 7% read at grade level in eighth grade.

Student educational attainment in Chicago, as elsewhere in Illinois and in the country at large, is also sharply divided by income. The city's schools teach 60% of students from families ineligible for subsidized meals to read proficiently, but only do this for 19% of students from eligible families. More than a third of the latter are left functionally illiterate. But this is only part of the story, because in Chicago, class equates to race: so much so that there are too few White students in the Chicago public schools from families living in or near poverty, and therefore eligible for the National Lunch Program, for NAEP to report a reading assessment for that group. Seventy-five percent of other White students, those from more prosperous families, are taught to read at grade level in Chicago's middle schools. Reciprocally, there are too few Black students from more prosperous families for NAEP to report their test results. Among the other Black students, that vast majority from lower-income families, just 13% are taught in their middle schools to read at grade level and nearly half are left functionally illiterate. A White student from a comparatively prosperous family in Chicago—that is,

171

nearly any White, non-Hispanic, student—is between five and six times as likely to be brought to grade level in eighth grade reading than is a Black student, who is practically inevitably from a lower-income family.

Again, all of this data is much worse for male Black students in Chicago, 94% of those who are eligible for the National Lunch Program read below grade level in middle school and more than half of whom are left functionally illiterate by their schools.

How bad are Chicago's schools for African-American children? Some light can be thrown on that question by comparing the situation of Black students in Chicago's schools with that of Black students in the schools of West Virginia, that proverbially impoverished state. A Black middle school student in West Virginia is much more likely to be taught to read proficiently than a Black student in Chicago. Twenty percent of African-American eighth grade students in West Virginia read at grade level, compared to just 13% in Chicago. The racial gap in reading proficiency is 50 percentage points in Chicago, just eight in West Virginia. Fewer Black adults in West Virginia than in Chicago leave school without a high school diploma. The unemployment rate for African-Americans in West Virginia is much lower than that in Chicago and average family income is higher.

The Chicago Public Schools are not only challenged by the schools of wealthy suburbs, the education they provide to Black students is challenged, and surpassed, by those of Appalachia. The Chicago Public Schools can educate the great majority of White students so that they are "college- and career-ready." They educate only a small minority of Black students to that standard.

A study by the Council of State Governments Justice Center has established that school discipline practices are a good indicator of racial prejudice by the adults in the schools. The researchers found that disciplinary actions by teachers and school administrators for "attitude" and such were much more likely against African-American than White or Hispanic students. As with crime statistics, which measure police and prosecutor activity, not the activities of those arrested, so school discipline data is a measure of the activities and attitudes of teachers and administrators, not students. This can be seen in Chicago, where last year the rate of out-of-school suspensions for African-American students was 16 per 100 students, that for White students was 2 per 100 students. Out-of-school suspensions have been shown to be an efficient method of persuading students to leave school without a diploma. In light of the fact that some students were given more than one out-of-school suspension, a total of ten percent of the district's individual Black students were given out-of-school suspensions, as were just two percent of the district's White students. The data for male students was even more dramatic: Eleven percent of male Black students and just two percent of male White students were given out-of-school suspensions. Working from the Justice Center findings, we could construct a "racial prejudice index" based on these differences in discipline rates. If we did, it would stand as five to one against Black students in the Chicago public schools.

That is how things work on a day-to-day, school-level basis in the Chicago public schools. Only a few African-American students are taught to read as well as White students; many more African-American students are "disciplined" than White students, and in this way encouraged to leave school before graduation. A third of them do just that. Of those who do graduate, few are college- and career-ready. As a consequence, Black family incomes are low, poverty (and incarceration) rates are high, the life-chances of the next generation poor.

There are similar factors on the "structural" level of school finance. The pupil/teacher ratio in the Chicago schools is 24:1 in elementary school and 22:1 in the high schools. The state averages are lower: 19:1 in both. If Chicago's schools were staffed at the state average it would mean an additional teacher for every four elementary school classrooms, and one more for every six high school classrooms.

Just over the Chicago city-line, in Evanston, the pupil/teacher ratio is 15:1 and the average salary teacher salary is $79,000. If Chicago's schools were staffed and funded at the level of Evanston's it would mean an additional teacher for every other classroom and that the amount spent on teacher salaries for those two classrooms would be $237,000, rather than $140,000. Of course Evanston is not nearly the wealthiest school district in Illinois. The teachers in the Adlai E. Stevenson High School District, for example, are paid, on average, $92,000 per year.

NAEP reports 24% of Chicago's eighth grade students reading at grade level. It does not report results for Evanston. However, for a comparison of how well Evanston and Chicago educate their students we can refer to the Illinois Report Card. Using state test results, the Illinois Report Card tells us that 30% of Chicago's eighth grade students met or exceeded "expectations" in English Language Arts. In Evanston, students did so at a rate of 43%, nearly 50% higher than in Chicago. The state's "expectations" are apparently lower than NAEP's, but the relative standings of Evanston and Chicago are clear enough.

Now, Evanston is a small city, where two-thirds of adults are college graduates (and more than one-third have advanced degrees) and the median household income is over $70,000. It would seem natural that teachers there would be better paid than those in Chicago, that class sizes would be markedly smaller, that educational achievement would be very much better. Natural, also, that just 1% of students met state achievement expectations at Manley High School in Chicago's East Garfield Park, with its almost entirely Black, and lower-income, student enrollment. But, on second thought, what is "natural" about that? Why are Illinois's schools financed in such a way as to provide the most resources for those who need them least, the fewest resources for those who need them most, which, as it happens, plays out as the divide between White and African-American students? Schools could be financed in other ways. Of course those other ways would not necessarily result in racial disparities.

The system in Chicago is failing African-American children. But if a system fails in its professed purpose—say, educating children— more often than chance would indicate, and continues to do so over time, it is probable that it is, in fact, achieving its actual purpose, in this case, perpetuating racism. This is not the responsibility of some disembodied "structure," it is the responsibility of specific individuals. If the governor and the legislators of Illinois wished to

174

change the system of school finance, they could do so. That they do not change it makes them responsible for the enormous, race-based, inequities in the resources available to schools children in the state. Given the importance of Chicago in Illinois, the injustices in the state can also be traced to the mayor of that city. More directly, the nearly incredible inequities within the Chicago public schools are attributable to his actions (and inactions) and those of the chief executive officer of the Chicago Public Schools. If they wished to educate African-American children in Chicago, let us say, at least as well as those of West Virginia, they could do so. When will they take up the West Virginia challenge?

Three-Fifths of an Education

New York and New Jersey

One in ten American descendants of enslaved Africans live in the wealthy, neighboring, mid-Atlantic states of New York and New Jersey. If we just look at the education provided for middle class Black students in suburban New Jersey, things there are not so bad. According to the National Assessment of Educational Progress, nearly a third of these students read at or above grade level in middle school. This is more than double the national average for Black students and not all that much lower than the 42% national average for White, non-Hispanic, students. If not quite half full, that glass is only a little more than half empty. There is, however, another issue to consider: How many students are we talking about? Of the 225,694 Black students in New Jersey's public schools, 558 are enrolled in what the NICHE website classifies as the state's ten best suburban school districts. That is two-tenths of one percent. There are 15,479 Black students in eighth grade in the state, 57 of whom are enrolled in those ten suburban school districts. Perhaps all of them are reading at grade level. That would be three-tenths of one percent.

There are other suburbs in the state, not among "the ten best." In some of these there are Black students whose family incomes are low enough to qualify them for free- or reduced-price meals. Fourteen percent of those students from impoverished suburban Black families read proficiently in eighth grade, the same proportion as those Black students eligible for the National Lunch Program in the cities. (According to NAEP there are too few middle class Black students in New Jersey's cities for whom to report test scores.)

If we concentrate on the success of those very few middle class suburban Black students, we miss the main story. The vast majority of Black students in New Jersey live in cities and are from relatively impoverished families. Public schools in New Jersey do not teach nearly 90% of them to read proficiently by the time they are in middle school.

The situation is similar in the state of New York. Of the 492,373 Black students in that state's public schools, 438 are enrolled in what the NICHE website classifies as the state's ten best suburban school districts. Of the 36,182 New York State Black eighth graders, 35 are enrolled in those "best" school districts. It is not then surprising that according to NAEP there are too few middle class Black students in the New York suburbs to meet the organization's statistical reporting standards. As a matter of fact, there are too few Black students at *any* income level in the state's suburbs for NAEP to report on their levels of educational achievement. So we don't know how those students are doing. Perhaps they are doing very well. Perhaps not. In any case, it hardly matters in the great scheme of things how well New York State's schools educate less than one-tenth of one percent of their Black students. Or two-tenths of one percent. Or even four-tenths of one percent.

It should be noted here that there are more than seventy African and Caribbean countries with representatives at the United Nation's in New York City. Some of their diplomats may have children. Some of those children may be in suburban schools in New York and New Jersey. They probably do well.

While ten percent of White adults in New Jersey and New York do not have high school diplomas, the percentages for Black adults are 14% in New Jersey and nearly twice as high as that for White, non-Hispanics, 19%, in New York. Thirty-seven percent of White adults in both states have Bachelor's degrees or higher, but only 21% of Black adults in these states have attained this increasingly necessary qualification. The unemployment rates of Black residents of New Jersey and New York are twice those of White residents. The average incomes of Black residents of New Jersey and New York are about three-fifths of those of White residents and, of course, the poverty rates are twice as high. The occupations of the White population in these states tend to be in management, business, science and the arts, while Black workers are much more likely than White workers to be employed in service occupations.

Student educational attainment in New Jersey is sharply divided by income as well as by race. Among Black students, 14% of those eligible for the National Lunch Program read at or above the proficient level, while more than twice as many, 32%, of those from more prosperous families do so. The situation is different in New York State. There, 16% of Black students eligible for the National Lunch Program read at or above the proficient level, while only slightly more as many, 20%, of those from more prosperous families do so. The source of this problem appears to be New York State's cities. Nationally, there is a ten percentage point gap between the percentage of Black students in city schools reading at grade level in eighth grade who are eligible for the National Lunch Program and those reading at grade level who come from more prosperous families: 12% to 22%. In New York State that gap is only three percentage points: 16% to 19%. While the state's urban schools do somewhat better than the national averages for impoverished Black students, they do worse, by the same amount, for middle class Black students. This is not the case for White, non-Hispanic, students, for whom both New York State groups the percentage reading at grade level is a few points higher than the national average for White students in grade eight. (Nor is it the case for Hispanic students.) In other words, opportunities in urban schools in the state of New York are primarily determined by the race of their students, with economic class having less to do with it than is the usual case nationally or in neighboring New Jersey.

While a Black student from a comparatively prosperous family in New Jersey is much more likely to read at or above grade level at eighth grade than a White student in that state who is eligible for the National Lunch Program, a Black student from a comparatively prosperous family in New York is unlikely to read at or above grade level at eighth grade more often than a White student eligible for the National Lunch Program. The narrow difference in educational achievement by family income for Black students in New York reflects the extreme residential segregation and poor quality of schools attended by Black students in the state. This problem is concentrated in New York City, which has two-thirds of the state's

179

Black population. In New York City, the gap between eligible and ineligible White students is 21 percentage points but that between eligible and ineligible Black students is just four points. (This is not about "people of color." The Hispanic income-based gap in New York City is 12 points.) In the New York metropolitan statistical area (New York city and three suburban counties), the average Black student attends a school in which 79% of the students are poor and the segregation index is 82, where 60 is considered very high.

In these wealthy states, 69% of middle class suburban New Jersey middle school Black students, 81% of New York urban middle class Black students, and 85% of Black students living in or near poverty in those states, are so ill-served by their schools as to be unable to read at grade level in middle school. More than a third of Black students in New Jersey and approaching half of the Black students in New York's eighth grade classes test at NAEP's Below Basic level: they are functionally illiterate.

The education levels of adults have implications for children. Cultural capital is transmitted within families from one generation to another, much like investments or houses, for those who have them. The children of musicians are favorably positioned to become musicians, of artists to become artists, of college professors to become educators, of real estate developers . . . well, we had better leave that one alone. In any case, in New York and New Jersey, higher levels of parental education are associated with higher levels of student achievement for both Black and White students. To begin with, NAEP has not been able to identify any students in those states, Black or White, who read at grade level in middle school, whose parents did not complete high school. And at the other end of the educational scale, more than half of the White students whose parents are college graduates *were* able to read at least at grade level in eighth grade. But the effect is much weaker for Black students. Less than a quarter of Black students whose parents graduated from college read proficiently in middle school and are therefore likely to graduate from high school and go on to college themselves. The educational ladder, such as it is, in New York and New Jersey is shorter for the descendants of enslaved Africans.

Why is that? Or, rather, how do officials in New Jersey and New York accomplish these racially disparate outcomes?

One strategy is implemented at the grassroots: school discipline practices. New York State teachers, school and district administrators and others impose out-of-school suspensions on Black students twice as often as on White students. In New Jersey they do this four times as often. Students who are removed from school by their teachers, counselors and principals, even briefly, are likely later to remove themselves, or be removed, from education entirely. When this happens, when these students "drop-out," the path of responsibility often can be traced to those teachers, counselors and principals who inflicted out-of-school suspensions or expulsions and to the higher officials who created those policies and tolerate, or encourage, those practices.

At the school district level, the educational opportunities of Black students in New Jersey and New York are limited by the legislative practice of creating large numbers of small districts with cleverly drawn boundaries. This facilitates allocating superior educational resources to predominately White communities and neighborhoods. There are more than one hundred school districts on New York's Long Island alone, averaging five schools each. In contrast, Long Island has only two counties for governance purposes. The proper functioning of local democratic institutions requires two counties; the race-based distribution of educational resources requires over a hundred school districts. There are six hundred school districts in New Jersey, averaging four schools each and there are just 21 counties. Some of these districts are nearly all White, others serve relatively few students who are not Black, Hispanic, or impoverished Whites. In both states (and elsewhere in this country) school district segregation reflects and maintains residential segregation. The Brown University's Dissimilarity Index for Blacks and Whites in the New York-Northern New Jersey-Long Island Metropolitan area is 77. In New York City itself the index of residential segregation is 81, in Newark, 71. (In the historically Jim Crow Birmingham, Alabama, metropolitan area it is 65; in Atlanta, 58.)

Three-Fifths of an Education

In a 2016 article about the case of *Abbott v. Burke* (1990) *The New York Times* wrote that the state's Supreme Court had ruled "that New Jersey was bound by the State Constitution to fund districts at a level that allows all children to receive an education that enables them to participate in the economy and a democratic society." It went on to observe that "The state's current funding formula . . . begins by determining the cost of educating a typical student, and then adds amounts for educating English language learners, poor children and so on . . .

> A 2013 study of children who had participated in Abbott District preschool programs showed that they made significant gains in literacy, language, math and science through the fourth and fifth grades. Beyond that, a national study published by the National Bureau of Economic Research found that court-ordered spending increases led to higher graduation rates, higher adult earnings, higher family incomes and fewer in poverty for those who had benefited as children (*The New York Times,* June 26, 2016, p. SR 10).

In spite of *Abbott,* and a less successfully implemented law with similar intent in New York State, residential segregation and the small size and homogeneous populations of many districts in New Jersey and New York make it easy for state officials to design policies that limit educational resources and opportunities for Black students. This situation seems to be getting worse. In New Jersey, the Education Law Center has found that "The weighted per pupil funding gap between the highest and lowest poverty districts has risen from $873 per pupil in 2008-09, to $3,875 per pupil in the current (2016-17) school year. While the lowest poverty districts [i.e., richest] received only 8% more funding than the highest in 2008-09, they now receive 40% more."

A particularly overt action by an official in New Jersey to limit educational opportunities for Black and other impoverished students was undertaken by then-Governor Christie in June, 2016. According to *The New York Times*, the Governor planned to provide "a uniform amount of $6,599 per student in state aid to all districts, with an exemption that would provide more money for special education students." *The Times* commented:

While it sounds reasonable, a flat amount would make it impossible for poor communities to provide a sound education for disadvantaged children who need classrooms with more resources. The state is required by law to send more money to those communities because they simply don't have the tax base or property values to raise additional revenues on their own . . . the proposal would gut the Newark school system, which relies on the state for about 85 percent of its budget. The district would have to cut more than half of its budget, which would clearly mean firing staff and shuttering schools. Wealthier districts would, meanwhile, get more state aid so they could cut local property taxes (*The New York Times,* June 26, 2016, p. SR 10).

Fortunately, this action was blocked.

New Jersey officials reported to the U.S. Department of Education that its graduation rate for the 2014-15 school year was 82% for Black students (the national rate was 75%). Given that only 20% of New Jersey's Black students were reading at grade level in 2011, it appears that three-quarters of graduating Black students in New Jersey received their diplomas while having serious deficiencies in their reading skills, that is, unable to read as well as required of a middle school student. New York reported graduating two-thirds of its Black students, while only 18% of Black students were reading at grade level in 2011, when they were in eighth grade. It appears, then, that more than three-quarters of graduating Black students in New York as well received their diplomas while having serious deficiencies in their reading skills.

If Black children in New Jersey were educated as well as White, non-Hispanic, children, 8,300, rather than the current 2,400 would graduate college- and career-ready each year. If Black children in New York were educated as well as White, non-Hispanic, children, 20,000, rather than the current 4.300 would graduate college- and career-ready each year.

Three-Fifths of an Education

Focus: New York City

Among the northern urban centers, New York City, because of its size and cultural and political significance, is of particular importance. New York City has by far the largest Black population among the nation's cities, 2,089,000, a quarter of the city's residents. Those two million African-American New York City residents, by and large, still live in another country from many others in the city, a country more closely resembling the lesser developed areas of the global south than that of the highly developed areas of northern Europe or White America. New York City's Black families are not only considerably poorer than the city's White families, something we have become accustomed to taking for granted, but should not, but they are poorer than the average American family and twice as many live in poverty as both the national average for all races as well as the local average for White families. They live in another country.

Given that background, we now turn to a consideration of how well the New York City public schools, specifically, do in their task of educating all children, including all Black children, for education is the doorway, the magic carpet, from poverty to prosperity. Or so it is said.

The National Assessment of Educational Progress results for eighth grade reading for New York City show that 46% of White students are proficient and above (compared to 42% nationally) as are just 15% of Black students. Forty-four percent of Black students in the city's middle schools, but "only" 15% of White students were at the Below Basic level in 2015, functionally illiterate. Thus, NAEP tells us that New York City's public schools teach three times the percentage of their White students as their Black students to read at grade level in the crucial eighth grade year. And that they leave nearly half of Black middle school students able to read only with difficulty, therefore unlikely to graduate from high school "college and career ready," unlikely to qualify for or to obtain middle class jobs and incomes. The failure of the New York City public schools to educate Black students is particularly troubling for male Black students, only 9% of whom are at proficient or above in eighth grade reading in 2015. Which means, of course, that 91% are not.

Much educational data is presented with reference to the eligibility of the family of students for free- or reduced-price lunch, as a rough indicator of economic class. Three-quarters of the White families in New York City have higher incomes than that cut-off. It is just below the mid-point for New York City's Black family incomes. In New York City, 36% of White students from families living in or near poverty, and therefore eligible for the National Lunch Program reach the proficient and above levels in eighth grade reading. Fifty-seven percent of other White students, those from more prosperous families, read at grade level in eighth grade. A White student from a comparatively prosperous family in New York is more than four times as likely to be brought to grade level in eighth grade reading as a Black student from a low-income family. Among Black students, 13% of those eligible for the National Lunch Program read at or above the proficient level, while just 18% of those from more prosperous families do so, a remarkably small gap for income within race. The close alignment of lower and middle income Black reading proficiency in New York City reflects the extreme segregation of the city's schools and the low quality of those serving Black students.

The gap between students from relatively poor and relatively prosperous families in New York City is 21 percentage points among White students, just five among Black students. NAEP's records for New York City assessments of this type go back only to 2003, but, nevertheless, if we look at those, we find that the family-income-based NAEP differences for White students are pretty steady, over time, but for Black students they are narrowing, from 13 percentage points in 2007 to those five percentage points in 2015. The reading ability of New York City's Black middle class students is declining, according to NAEP, while that of Black students from lower-income families is not improving.

How can this be interpreted? New York is one of the nation's most segregated cities, as are its schools. While since the Lyndon Johnson administration formal housing segregation has been illegal, in New York City even middle class Black professionals are *de facto* ghettoized. Therefore, by and large, their children go to the same schools as do the children of the poorest, single-parent, families. In theory, this should not matter. In theory, all schools would provide educations of equal—high—quality to all students.

It is obvious that all but 15% of Black children (and 9% of male Black children) in New York City are being provided with inferior educational opportunities because they are Black, without regard to the economic class of their families. And of those, comparatively successful students, many are the children of school teachers and other highly educated parents, in effect, home schooled: the home environment making up for the deficiencies of the school (rather than the idealized opposite). The racism of the New York City public school system is more or less overt, as witness the unspeakable racial imbalance of the system's selective high schools, which year after year admit so few Black students that those could be accounted for by the number of children of those Black United Nations diplomats. The outcome of all this is that the 65% of Black students entering grade 9 in New York City who were given diplomas four years later include about 40% who could not read at grade level when they were in eighth grade and probably could not read eighth grade material when they were given diplomas. More than one-third of the system's Black students do not graduate from high school, two-thirds or more of those who do are far from "college and career ready."

In the 2013-14 school year, 3% of Black students in New York City and 0.5% of White students were given at least one out-of-school suspension.[58] Those who are responsible for the education of children and who decide one day to allocate fewer certified teachers to a school predominately attended by Black students and another day decide not to provide alternatives to out-of-school suspensions and expulsions; those who propose allocating more funding to schools attended by middle class and upper middle class (White) children and less to schools attended by Black students; those who, faced with a situation where selective secondary schools select out Black students, do nothing, are each responsible for perpetuating the conditions under which Black children receive three-fifths, or less, of the educational opportunities of White children.

If a system fails in its professed purpose—say, educating all children—more often than chance would indicate, and continues to do so over time, it is probable that it is, in fact, achieving its actual purpose, in this case, perpetuating racism.

Three-Fifths of an Education

Ohio

Ohio, with its seemingly endless miles of cornfields and a culturally as well as geographically southern area along the Ohio River, was also one of the more important industrial states of the twentieth century. Its manufacturing plants along Lake Erie were among the principal destinations of the Great Migration of the descendants of enslaved Africans from the Jim Crow former slave states. Today, even though Ohio has a slightly below average percentage of African-American residents (12%), it still has among the larger Black populations in terms of absolute numbers (1.4 million).

A much larger proportion of Ohio's Black students than of the state's White, non-Hispanic, students are from families with incomes low enough to make them eligible for the National Lunch Program. While just one-third of White, non-Hispanic, families meet the eligibility requirement for a family of four, most—55%—of Black families have incomes low enough to be eligible for free- and reduced-price meals. At the extremes, 15% of Black families have incomes under $10,000 per year, as compared to just 4% of White families, and 24% of White families have incomes over $100,000 per year, as compared to10% of Black families. Half of Ohio families with incomes under $10,000 per year are Black—four times as many as would be expected from their share in the population; on the other hand, just 5% of families with incomes over $100,000 in Ohio are Black.

Although the poverty rate for White, non-Hispanic, residents of the state is better than the national average for that group, that for Black residents of Ohio, at 28%, is worse than the national average for African-Americans and, of course, much worse than that of White, non-Hispanics. By these and most other measures, Black residents of the state are worse off than White, non-Hispanic, residents. This is not surprising, but it should not be taken for granted as somehow natural. It did not just happen. It followed from over a century of decisions by state and local officials, decisions by governors and state legislators and school district superintendents and members of boards of education. Nor do these racial disparities just happen to continue. They are caused by today's decisions by state and local officials: from the governor and state legislators to school district superintendents and members of boards of education.

Although some Ohio school districts were segregated until the *Brown* decision, none are now *legally* racially segregated. However, school segregation continues in Ohio, as elsewhere, arising now from housing and economic segregation rather than explicit laws. The degree of the segregation of many of Ohio's schools is apparent if we use the Brown University Index of Dissimilarity data for Cincinnati in the south of the state and Cleveland in the northeast. The Index, a measure of segregation, has a reading of 63 for the Cincinnati school district and 70 for Cleveland, where 60 or above is considered very high. In Ohio only 9% of Black students are in districts where the White, non-Hispanic, enrollment is 75% or more. In other words, over 90% of Black students in Ohio are in districts that are perceived as being in varying degrees "Black districts." On the other hand, if we define districts with less than 5% White, non-Hispanic, enrollment as "intensely segregated," we find that there are more than 36,000 African-American students (out of 280,000) in such intensely segregated districts.

The provision of high quality pre-school education is a proven strategy for increasing educational achievement, especially for African-American children and those from lower-income homes. Unfortunately, Ohio makes little effort to provide high quality prekindergarten education, enrolling just 8% of its 4-year-olds (and 3% of its 3-year-olds) in the state's programs. As a result, Ohio ranks 33rd in the country for access to preschool programs for four-year-olds according to the National Institute for Early Education Research, and 27th for state spending on preschool. The need for initiatives such as high quality preschool, for the most part lacking in Ohio, is illustrated by the fact that more than half of the African-

American fourth graders eligible for the National Lunch Program test at the Below Basic level on the National Assessment of Educational Progress. On the other hand, over half of White, non-Hispanic, fourth graders from middle class families test at or above grade level, which indicates that the state's schools can teach young children to read; they simply do not offer most young Black children that opportunity.

The National Assessment of Educational Progress results for eighth grade reading for Ohio are similar to the dismal national averages for that grade: just 14% of Black middle school students are taught to read proficiently, compared to 40% of White, non-Hispanic, students. And 45% of Black eighth graders are left virtually illiterate (as compared to 19% of White students). While outcomes by income for all of Ohio's middle school students are nearly the same as national averages (20% of lower-income students at grade level; 50% of middle class students reading proficiently), among Black students just 9% of those from lower-income families read at grade level. A White student from a comparatively prosperous family in Ohio is approximately five times as likely to be brought to grade level in eighth grade reading as a Black student from a low-income family.

Not teaching students to read effectively limits other educational opportunities in a fundamental way. They may never go to college, succeed in a training program, get a well-paid job. Another effective way to discourage students from completing their educations is to suspend or expel them for perceived disciplinary infractions. In the 2011-12 school year, nearly five times the percentage of Ohio's Black students (19%) as that of its White students (4%) were given at least one out-of-school suspension. This is arguably a measure of the degree of racial prejudice among the state's school-level administrators and teachers.

As a consequence, the 4-year adjusted cohort graduation rate reported by Ohio for the 2014-15 school year was 60% for Black students and 86% for White students. (The national graduate rates were 75% for Black students and 88% for White, non-Hispanic, students.) Given that only 14% of Black students and 40% of White

191

students were reading at grade level in 2011, when they were in eighth grade, it appears that only a fifth of Black students in Ohio and about half of White students received their diplomas while reading at grade 8 proficiency or better. On the other hand, if the state's Black students had the educational opportunities afforded its White, non-Hispanic, students, an additional 9,300 Black students would graduate career-and college-ready each year, up from the current 1,900.

Focus: Cleveland

We can look more closely at the educational opportunities allowed, or denied, African-American students in Ohio by looking at the situation in Cleveland, a city of 400,000 people at the center of a metropolitan area with a population of two million. Just over one-third of the residents of Cleveland are White, non-Hispanic, over half are Black. Cleveland's Black unemployment rate is twice that of the city's White unemployment rate. The median income of Black families in Cleveland is $27,451, that for White families it is $44,015. Thirty-nine percent of Black residents of the city have incomes below the poverty level, as compared to 21% of the White residents. A quite remarkable quarter (24%) of Black households in Cleveland have annual incomes of less than $10,000, twice the proportion of such severely impoverished White households in the city, and more than half of Black households have incomes below the poverty level. While 9% of White households have incomes over $100,000, only 2% of Black households in Cleveland have incomes at that level. The percentage of Black households in Cleveland with incomes over $150,000 rounds to zero.

Intergenerational economic mobility is a key measure of equity. The average income of U.S. White families in the highest income quintile (20%) is nearly 30 times that of Black families in the lowest quintile. The poorest Black families are relatively twice as poor as the poorest White families, with the poorest Black families in Cleveland even worse off than the national average. More than half of Black families in Cleveland have incomes in the lowest quintile of the national income distribution. As we have seen, Cleveland is a highly segregated city with a Brown University Black/White dissimilarity index of 70. The metropolitan area has an even higher dissimilarity index: 73. The US Schools Project at Brown University has found that the average Black student in the district is in a school where 87% of the students are poor. Fewer than 600 Black students in Cleveland are in schools 25% or less Black; 14,000 out of 25,000 are in schools 95% or more Black. Raj Chetty and his colleagues have calculated that the chance of a child in Cleveland born to parents with incomes in the bottom 20% (that is, more than half the

193

Black population of the city) reaching the top 20% are as low as any in the country, less than 5%.

Cleveland is one of the districts analyzed for educational achievement by the National Assessment of Educational Progress. Two-thirds of African-American fourth grade students in Cleveland test at the Below Basic level, that is, for most intents and purposes they are unable to read. Over 90% of the district's Black fourth graders have not reached proficiency in reading. These results at the end of the primary grades are much worse than the national averages. Nonetheless, the district passes these students on to the upper primary and middle school grades. In eighth grade, over half of the district's Black students still test as functionally illiterate and over 90% of the district's Black middle school students have not reached proficiency in reading. (The State Department of Education of Ohio, to its credit, has faced this dismal reality and given the district a grade of F in each of its evaluative categories.) Cleveland's four-year graduation rate for the 2015-6 school year was 69%. The state's "Prepared for Success" measure is the "number of students that [sic] earned a remediation free score on all parts of the ACT or SAT," expressed as a percentage of the cohort. Cleveland's score was 6.5%. Just 8.5% of the 2009 graduating class graduated from college within six years of leaving high school. These are percentages that probably would not be much, if at all, worse if there was no school district in Cleveland; if children in that city did not go to school at all.

Arguably, the cause of generation after generation of poverty in Ohio's African-American families is their lack of educational opportunities and a reason for that is the inequitable distribution of educational resources in the state. "White districts" tend to be better resourced than "Black districts" in Ohio, as elsewhere in the United States. For example, average teacher salaries in the Hilliard City public school district (a large suburb of Columbus), with a 75% White, non-Hispanic, enrollment, are $74,000, while in Cleveland, average teachers salaries are $66,700 and average teacher experience is 11 years, as compared to 15 years in Hilliard. Eighty-one percent of teachers in Hilliard are evaluated as "Accomplished," the highest category, as compared to 27% in Cleveland, where just 2% of principals are evaluated as "Accomplished," as compared to 97% in

Hilliard. As can be seen from these examples, Black students in Ohio attend schools with fewer "accomplished," experienced teachers, hardly any "accomplished" principals and lower salaries all around for their educators. A "Dear Colleague" letter from the U.S. Assistant Secretary of Education for Civil Rights of October 1, 2014, noted that the "Chronic and widespread racial disparities in access to rigorous courses, academic programs, and extracurricular activities; stable workforces of effective teachers, leaders, and support staff; safe and appropriate school buildings and facilities; and modern technology and high-quality instructional materials further hinder the education of students of color today." This inequitable distribution of resources is a major cause of the failure of the Cleveland Metropolitan School District to educate Black students.

* * *

Who is responsible for the failure to educate the overwhelming majority of Ohio's Black students, children whose futures have been entrusted to the state? Each district has a board of education—Cleveland's is appointed by the city's mayor—and a superintendent. They are responsible. There is a State Board of Education, with 19 members, eight who are appointed by the governor. They are responsible. Mayors and the governor; members of city councils, the state legislature and boards of education; district superintendents; they are each and every one individually and collectively responsible and they have failed to meet that responsibility.

Three-Fifths of an Education

Pennsylvania

Pennsylvania, with its Quaker traditions, was a center of the anti-slavery movement, part of the route of the Underground Railroad, among the principal destinations of the Great Migration of the descendants of enslaved Africans from the Jim Crow former slave states of the south: an early center of American civilization. Times have changed. Today, only half the proportion of African-American adults in Pennsylvania as that of White, non-Hispanic, adults have attained a Bachelor's degree or higher (17% to 31%). A much larger percentage of Pennsylvania's Black residents than White residents have left school without a high school diploma (15% to 9%). A much higher percentage of White residents than Black residents are employed in managerial occupations and a much higher percentage of Black residents than White are employed in service occupations. Black family incomes are both much lower than those of White families in the state and lower than the national average for African-Americans. The poverty rate for the 1.4 million Black residents of Pennsylvania is more than triple that for White Pennsylvanians.

These matters are all connected. Adults, particularly Black adults, without a high school diploma have little chance for middle class careers, those without college degrees little chance of securing jobs in the professions. Children whose parents have not graduated from college have less of a chance to do well in school than those whose parents are well-educated. By failing to close the gaps in both the amount and quality of educational opportunities between Black and White residents of Pennsylvania, its state and local officials ensure that what amounts to a racially-based caste system in Pennsylvania will remain in place.

High quality prekindergarten programs have positive effects that continue to be evident through the primary grades. Pennsylvania is

197

ranked 30th for access to prekindergarten for 4-year olds by the National Institute for Early Education Research. Perhaps in part because of this limited access, Pennsylvania's early childhood education system does not have the expected positive results in the primary grades for Black children, just 15% of whom are in the state's prekindergarten classrooms. While 49% of its White, non-Hispanic, fourth-graders are taught to read at the level expected at that grade, only 17% of Pennsylvania's African-American fourth graders read at grade level. Pennsylvania's urban schools, especially, lag far behind national averages in teaching fourth grade students to read. While nationally 30% of urban children read at grade level in fourth grade, Pennsylvania's urban schools successfully teach only 19% of their students to read proficiently in primary school, while the state's suburban schools teach more than half of their students to read well—approximately the same proportion who are left functionally illiterate in fourth grade by the state's urban schools. Much of the problem is traceable to Philadelphia, where just 10% of African-American students are taught to read proficiently in fourth grade, and even fewer, 8%, of Black children from lower-income families are taught to read to that grade level. In Philadelphia, over 90% of Black children from lower-income families do not reach grade level in reading and nearly two-thirds are functionally illiterate in fourth grade, as are more than half of Black children from middle class families.

Could more access to high quality prekindergarten classes improve this situation? Most researchers believe it would. Why, then, is it that 85% of Black children in the state are not given that opportunity?

Four more years in Pennsylvania's schools result in approximately the same proportion of White children reading at grade level in eighth grade as in fourth grade and a decline to 13% of Black students who are taught by their schools to read proficiently. The state's record for its White, non-Hispanic, students is better than the national average for the group (42%), while its record for its Black students is worse than the national average of 16%, bringing the state's racial gap to 34 percentage points, notably greater than the national gap of 27 percentage points, which is in itself, of course, unacceptable.

It is generally expected that education is an important aspect of cultural capital that is passed down within families. But positive attitudes toward education in the home in Pennsylvania seem to be overwhelmed by the lack of educational opportunities for Black students in the state's public schools. They teach nearly a third, 30%, of White, non-Hispanic, students whose parents did not progress beyond high school to read at the level expected in eighth grade. This is more than twice the percentage of the state's Black children of college graduates who are taught to read at grade level in middle school. In Pennsylvania, it is the color of your skin, without regard to the education level of your parents, that leads to educational opportunities.

Student educational attainment in Pennsylvania, as elsewhere in this country, is divided by income as well as by race. White students from families living in or near poverty, and therefore eligible for the National Lunch Program, read at grade level in eighth grade half as often as students from more prosperous White families in the state. Black students from families living in or near poverty, and therefore eligible for the National Lunch Program, read at grade level in eighth grade just under two-thirds as often in Pennsylvania as Black students from middle class families. The gap between Black students from poorer families and White students from prosperous families is more than forty percentage points. Family economic status matters much more for Pennsylvania's White, non-Hispanic, students than it does for the state's African-American students. The gap based on income among White students is approximately twenty points, among Black students it is just eight points. One explanation for this might be that higher family income in Pennsylvania does not protect Black students from relegation to inferior, segregated, schools.

Racial disparities in Pennsylvania compound those of economic class. The racial gap for students from lower-income families is 15 points in Pennsylvania, as it is nationally, but that for students from middle class families is 38 points, 14 points greater than the national average. A White student from a comparatively prosperous family in

Three-Fifths of an Education

Pennsylvania is approximately five times as likely to be brought to grade level in eighth grade reading as is a Black student from a low-income family. A Black student from a comparatively prosperous family in Pennsylvania is not as likely to read at or above grade level in eighth grade as is a White student from a lower-income family. In Pennsylvania, it is the color of your skin, not just the color of your money, that counts.

As in fourth grade, in eighth grade the lack of educational opportunities for African-American students is especially acute in Pennsylvania's urban districts. More than 90% of Black students from lower-income families in city schools are not taught to read at grade level in middle school and half are left functionally illiterate. Even middle class Black students are denied a meaningful education in the state's urban schools: just 12% are taught to read at grade level in eighth grade. It is not that the schools are unable to teach their students to read. Twenty percent of lower-income White students in city schools read proficiently in eighth grade, as do more than half of urban middle class White students. And in suburban schools nearly a third of lower-income and nearly two-thirds of middle class White students are taught to read proficiently. In Pennsylvania, it is the color of your skin, not just the location of your school, that counts.

The reality of the failure of the state's education system is partially hidden behind the inflated results reported by the Pennsylvania System of School Assessment (PSSA). The 2016 PSSA reported grade 8 English Language Arts at 58% Proficient and Advanced and 11% Below Basic. This compares with the NAEP results of 40% Proficient and above and 22% Below Basic. NAEP is considered "the gold standard" of education assessment. The PSSA does not meet that standard. The children of Pennsylvania are not well-served by an assessment system the reports from which conceal the deficiencies of their schools.

The study by the Council of State Governments Justice Center established that school discipline practices are a good indicator not of student behavior, but of the racial prejudices of the adults in the schools. The researchers found that disciplinary actions by teachers and school administrators for subjective issues, "attitude" and such, were much more likely to be used against African-American than

White or Hispanic students, while those for actions that can be objectively assessed, such as violence, were more evenly distributed among the racial and ethnic groups. As with crime statistics, which measure police and prosecutor activity, not simply the activities of those arrested, so school discipline data is a measure of the activities and attitudes of teachers and administrators, not just those of students. This can be seen in Pennsylvania, where more than five times the percentage of Black students (17%) as White students (3%) were given at least one out-of-school suspension.

We can note that it has been found that out-of-school suspensions, like expulsions, are an efficient way to discourage students from completing their educations.

The 4-year adjusted cohort graduation rate reported by Pennsylvania for the 2014-15 school year was 72% for Black students and 89% for White students. Given that only 14% of Black students and 41% of White students were reading at grade level in 2011, when they were in eighth grade, if we assume that all those who were proficient in middle school graduated, it appears that just 20% of Black students in Pennsylvania who began their high school education four years earlier and less than half of White students received their diplomas while reading at grade 8 proficiency or better. What are those diplomas worth? According to the College Board, in 2015 just 12% of Pennsylvania's African-American SAT takers met the SAT College and Career Readiness Benchmark. Of course, only those students considering college take the SAT so that it is quite possible that the percentage of the state's Black students graduating College and Career ready is much lower than that. If Pennsylvania educated its Black students as well as it educates its White, non-Hispanic, students, more than three times as many as at present would graduated college- and career-ready, more than 7,000 additional Black students each year.

Two-thirds of African-Americans in the state of Pennsylvania live in just three counties: Philadelphia, neighboring Delaware and Allegheny County (Pittsburgh). The responsibility for the catastrophic educational failure of the schools in the state can be

Three-Fifths of an Education

attributed to the administrations of the districts in those counties, particularly Philadelphia and Pittsburgh.

Focus on Philadelphia

The National Assessment of Educational Progress tracks data from the Philadelphia schools. Given that, and the plurality of the state's Black students in that district, we will focus on its provision of educational opportunities for the descendents of enslaved Africans as an indicator of the effort of the state as a whole. This is particularly apt as Philadelphia was a center of abolitionist sentiment and activity long before the Civil War. Today, nearly half (44%) of its residents are African-Americans. They are not doing well. The city's Black population of 672,000 has an unusually low percentage of highly educated adults, a very high percentage of adults without high school diplomas, a low median family income and a high unemployment rate.

Three-quarters of Philadelphia's Black families have incomes below the average for White families in the city. The poverty rate for Black families in Philadelphia is more than twice that of White families. At the other end of the income spectrum, nearly a third of Philadelphia's White families have incomes over $100,000 per year, as compared to just 11 percent of Black families. This may reflect the fact, among other things, that 44 percent of White civilian employed adults work in the managerial group of occupations, compared to 27 percent of Black civilian employed adults. Thirty-two percent of employed Black adults work in service occupations, as compared to 17 percent of employed White adults: in Philadelphia, Whites manage, Blacks serve. It is unlikely that there is much inter-generational family income or wealth upward mobility in Philadelphia's Black community. Raj Chetty and his colleagues calculate that the chances of a child born into a family in the bottom 20% of the national income distribution has less than a 5% chance of achieving an income in the top 20%. Black Philadelphia does not participate in the same society as White Philadelphia. It is a caste apart.

The Philadelphia public school district has a long history of conflicts between teachers and administrators, from elementary schools where principals lock themselves in their offices rather than meet with teachers to prolonged disputes between the teachers' union and the district administration. Spending on support services has trailed inflation. Non-teaching staff, such as counselors and librarians, have been severely cut. Many schools have been closed. The district has privatized its substitute teacher program, with initial disastrous results, although that situation has stabilized and it is now said to be no worse than before privatization, as if that were an achievement to be proud of.

The budgetary issues and administrative policies of the state and district are both complex and controversial, but there is little dispute over the record of the Philadelphia school district in teaching its students how to read. For most intents and purposes Philadelphia's schools fail to teach half of the district's middle class Black students in the primary grades to read and two-thirds of those from lower-income families. Just 15% of the district's Black students from middle class homes and 8% of those from lower-income homes learn to read proficiently in fourth grade. Four more years of schooling in the city's schools change little. The National Assessment of Educational Progress results for eighth grade reading for Philadelphia show that Philadelphia's public schools educate nearly three times the percentage of their White students as their Black students to read at grade level in the crucial eighth grade year. (26% of White students are proficient and above as compared to only 9% of Black students.) Twice the percentage of African-American students as White, non-Hispanic, students in the public schools were functionally illiterate in the eighth grade, a group that amounts to half of the Black students in that grade.

The district is able to help 14% of White students from families living in or near poverty to reach the proficient level in eighth grade reading. More than one-thirds of other eighth grade White students, those from more prosperous families, also read at grade level. But among Black students, it leaves over 90% of those eligible for the National Lunch Program unable to read proficiently, and only 12% of those from more prosperous families are given the opportunity to read at grade level. A White student from a comparatively prosperous family in Philadelphia is more than four times as likely to be brought to grade level in eighth grade reading as is a Black student from a lower-income family.

The 4-year adjusted cohort graduation rate reported by Philadelphia for the 2015-16 school year was 64% for Black students and 68% for White students.[59] Given that only 12% of Black students and 37% of White students were reading at grade level in 2011, it appears that the great majority of graduating Black students in Philadelphia receive their diplomas while still having serious deficiencies in their reading skills.

The Philadelphia public schools do not educate any group of their students as well as national averages for that group. They fail to come anywhere near to providing the quality of education given to students in nearby districts. Although family income and parental education levels have some effect on student achievement, these simply define the task of the schools. The extent of these failures in Philadelphia is too great to be attributed to anything other than the quality of the schools themselves.

The professed mission of the School District of Philadelphia is to provide to "every child in Philadelphia an excellent public school education and ensure all children graduate from high school ready to succeed, fully engaged as a citizen of our world." Philadelphia's School Reform Commission, the equivalent of a board of education, has recently rated the district superintendent a "strong" leader.[60] Given that one-third of the district's Black students are not well-enough educated to graduate in four years and that few of those who are handed a diploma are able to read proficiently, few understand high school level mathematics and few have reasonable subject area knowledge, it is difficult to imagine what is meant by such a judgment.

Who is responsible? These people are responsible: The School Reform Commission of Philadelphia, controlled by the governor of the state, is responsible for the failure of the Philadelphia schools to educate most of its African-America students. (Likewise, the Superintendent and Board of Directors of the Pittsburgh Schools are responsible for its failure to educate most of its African-American students.) The state's Secretary of Education and the state Board of Education; the state legislature and the governor are responsible for the race-based allocation of educational opportunities throughout

Three-Fifths of an Education

Pennsylvania.   Most directly the governor and the two big-city
district superintendents should be held accountable for failing to
preparing all children so that they have the opportunity to succeed in
life.

Notes

[1] U. S. Census, Selected Social Characteristics in the United States, 2006-2010 American Community Survey Selected Population Tables, DP02. Where not otherwise noted, data of this type can be found in this source.

[2] U.S. Department of Education, National Center for Education Statistics. Common Core of Data. Table 1. Public high school 4-year adjusted cohort graduation rate (ACGR). https://nces.ed.gov/ccd/tables/ACGR_RE_and_characteristics_2014-15.asp. Where not otherwise noted, data of this type can be found in this source.

[3] https://www.splcenter.org/news/2017/05/23/splc-suit-mississippi-violates-binding-obligation-provide-%E2%80%98uniform%E2%80%99-system-public-education

[4] U. S. Census, 2011-13 American Community Survey, 3-Year Estimates.

[5] http://www.equality-of-opportunity.org/neighborhoods/

[6] https://nces.ed.gov/programs/statereform/tab5_10.asp

[7] http://decal.ga.gov/Prek/Default.aspx

[8] http://ocrdata.ed.gov. Where not otherwise noted, data of this type can be found in this source.

[9] https://nces.ed.gov/programs/coe/indicator_coi.asp

[10] http://www.npr.org/sections/ed/2016/12/19/505729524/alabama-admits-its-high-school-graduation-rate-was-inflated

[11] U.S. Department of Education, National Center for Education Statistics. Common Core of Data. Table 1. Public high school 4-year adjusted cohort graduation rate (ACGR). https://nces.ed.gov/ccd/tables/ACGR_RE_and_characteristics_2014-15.asp. Where not otherwise noted, data of this type can be found in this source.

[12] http://www.privateschoolreview.com/alabama. Where not otherwise noted, data of this type can be found in this source.

[13] https://www.privateschoolreview.com/

[14] U. S. Census, Selected Social Characteristics in the United States, 2006-2010 American Community Survey Selected Population Tables, DP02.

[15] http://ocrdata.ed.gov/DataAnalysisTools/DataSetBuilder?Report=1

[16] U.S. Department of Education, National Center for Education Statistics. Common Core of Data. Table 1. Public high school 4-year adjusted cohort graduation rate (ACGR). https://nces.ed.gov/ccd/tables/ACGR_RE_and_characteristics_2014-15.asp

[17] U.S. Census, Public School System Finances. https://www.census.gov/govs/school/

[18] http://www.al.com/news/birmingham/index.ssf/2016/11/post_305.html

[19] http://www.teacherportal.com/teacher-salaries-by-state. Where not otherwise noted, data of this type can be found in this source.
[20]
http://www.al.com/news/index.ssf/2016/11/alabamas_school_finance_form ul.html, p. 31.
[21]
http://www.al.com/news/index.ssf/2016/11/alabamas_school_finance_form ul.html p. 27.
[22]
http://www.al.com/news/index.ssf/2016/11/alabamas_school_finance_form ul.html, p. 36.
[23] Raj Chetty, John N. Friedman, Jonah E. Rockoff. The Long-Term Impacts of Teachers: Teacher Value-Added and Student Outcomes in Adulthood. http://www.equality-of-opportunity.org/assets/documents/teachers_summary.pdf. Where not otherwise noted, data of this type can be found in this source.
[24] US Census, Selected Population Profile in the United States, 2011-2013 American Community Survey 3-Year Estimates.
[25] http://picardcenter.louisiana.edu/sites/picardcenter/files/ LA%204%20Annual%20Report%202007-08.pdf
[26] http://ocrdata.ed.gov/
[27] https://nces.ed.gov/programs/coe/indicator_coi.asp
[28] U. S. Census, Selected Social Characteristics in the United States, 2006-2010 American Community Survey Selected Population Tables, DP02.
[29] http://ocrdata.ed.gov/DataAnalysisTools/DataSetBuilder?Report=1
[30] U.S. Department of Education, National Center for Education Statistics. Common Core of Data. Table 1. Public high school 4-year adjusted cohort graduation rate (ACGR). https://nces.ed.gov/ccd/tables/ACGR_RE_and_characteristics_2014-15.asp. Where not otherwise noted, data of this type can be found in this source.
[31] US Census, Selected Population Profile in the United States, 2011-2013 American Community Survey 3-Year Estimates.
[32] U.S. Census, ACS 3-year Survey, 2011-13
[33] http://schoolgrades.fldoe.org/
[34] U.S. Census Bureau, Public Education Finances: 2015, G15-ASPEF, U.S. Government Printing Office, Washington, DC, 2017. Where not otherwise noted, data of this type can be found in this source.
[35] U. S. Census, Selected Social Characteristics in the United States, 2006-2010 American Community Survey Selected Population Tables, DP02.

[36] U. S. Census, Selected Social Characteristics in the United States, 2006-2010 American Community Survey Selected Population Tables, DP02.
[37] http://ocrdata.ed.gov/DataAnalysisTools/DataSetBuilder?Report=1
[38] http://ocrdata.ed.gov/DataAnalysisTools/DataSetBuilder?Report=1
[39] U.S. Department of Education, National Center for Education Statistics. Common Core of Data. Table 1. Public high school 4-year adjusted cohort graduation rate (ACGR).
https://nces.ed.gov/ccd/tables/ACGR_RE_and_characteristics_2014-15.asp
[40] U.S. Department of Education, National Center for Education Statistics. Common Core of Data. Table 1. Public high school 4-year adjusted cohort graduation rate (ACGR).
https://nces.ed.gov/ccd/tables/ACGR_RE_and_characteristics_2014-15.asp
[41] US Census, Selected Population Profile in the United States, 2011-2013 American Community Survey 3-Year Estimates.
[42] U. S. Census, Selected Social Characteristics in the United States, 2006-2010 American Community Survey Selected Population Tables, DP02.
[43] http://ocrdata.ed.gov/DataAnalysisTools/DataSetBuilder?Report=1
[44] U.S. Department of Education, National Center for Education Statistics. Common Core of Data. Table 1. Public high school 4-year adjusted cohort graduation rate (ACGR).
https://nces.ed.gov/ccd/tables/ACGR_RE_and_characteristics_2014-15.asp
[45] https://nces.ed.gov/programs/coe/indicator_coi.asp
[46] nces.ed.gov/programs/digest/d16/tables/dt16
[47] U.S. Census Bureau, *Public Education Finances: 2015*, G15-ASPEF, U.S. Government Printing Office, Washington, DC, 2017.
[48] http://ocrdata.ed.gov/DataAnalysisTools/DataSetBuilder?Report=2
[49] https://nces.ed.gov/programs/coe/indicator_coi.asp
[50] U. S. Census, Selected Social Characteristics in the United States, 2006-2010 American Community Survey Selected Population Tables, DP02.
[51] U. S. Census, Selected Social Characteristics in the United States, 2006-2010 American Community Survey Selected Population Tables, DP02.
[52] http://ocrdata.ed.gov/DataAnalysisTools/DataSetBuilder?Report=1
[53] http://ocrdata.ed.gov/DataAnalysisTools/DataSetBuilder?Report=1
[54] U.S. Department of Education, National Center for Education Statistics. Common Core of Data. Table 1. Public high school 4-year adjusted cohort graduation rate (ACGR).
https://nces.ed.gov/ccd/tables/ACGR_RE_and_characteristics_2014-15.asp
[55] U.S. Department of Education, National Center for Education Statistics. Common Core of Data. Table 1. Public high school 4-year adjusted cohort

graduation rate (ACGR).
https://nces.ed.gov/ccd/tables/ACGR_RE_and_characteristics_2014-15.asp
[56] https://nces.ed.gov/programs/statereform/tab5_10.asp
[57] https://nces.ed.gov/programs/coe/indicator_coi.asp
[58] http://ocrdata.ed.gov/DataAnalysisTools/DataSetBuilder?Report=1
[59] U.S. Department of Education, National Center for Education Statistics.
Common Core of Data. Table 1. Public high school 4-year adjusted cohort
graduation rate (ACGR).
https://nces.ed.gov/ccd/tables/ACGR_RE_and_characteristics_2014-15.asp
[60] http://www.philly.com/philly/blogs/school_files/Phila-superintendents-
job-evaluation-strong.html

APPENDIX

Three-Fifths of an Education

Urban Districts With Significant Black Populations

District	Total Students	Number Black Students	Percent Black Students
New York City	1,038,727	307,734	30%
Chicago	392,558	154,826	39%
Houston	215,225	90,122	42%
Miami-Dade	356,964	80,089	22%
Philadelphia	134,241	70,500	53%
Baltimore City	84,976	70,234	83%
Charlotte	145,636	58,887	40%
Los Angeles	646,683	56,863	9%
Duval County (FL)	128,685	56,507	44%
Hillsborough (FL)	207,469	44,402	21%
Milwaukee	77,316	42,232	55%
Detroit	47,277	39,257	83%
Atlanta	51,145	38,633	76%
Jefferson (KY)	100,602	36,911	37%
Dallas	160,253	36,621	23%
District of Col.	46,155	30,386	66%
Cleveland	39,365	25,915	66%
Boston	54,312	18,225	34%
Total/Average	3,927,589	1,258,344	45.72%

Three-Fifths of an Education

Charters

NAEP reports results for students enrolled in schools identified as "Charters," which it defines as "public schools of choice." Advocates of Charter schools range from those who originally proposed public schools in large districts independent from district requirements they thought harmful for education to those today advocating minimizing government at all levels and maximizing opportunities for private profits. Except for the latter, most Charter school advocates base their arguments on claimed superior outcomes for Charters as compared to other public schools. NAEP has made available assessments at the national level comparing Charters to other public schools. The following pages show the results of those assessments in regard to changes between 2003 and 2015 for all students and for the various subgroups. The conclusion to be drawn from these data is that there is little difference in outcomes for any group at any level, with a slight, but consistent, tendency for better outcomes for public schools students who are not enrolled in Charter schools.

All students: Fourth Grade
Between 2003 and 2015 there was little change in NAEP reading assessment results at fourth grade for students in non-Charter public schools, while there was some improvement for students in public Charter Schools. Nearly half, 42% of public Charter school students were classified as Below Basic in 2003, as were 38% of other students. A third, 34%, of public Charter school fourth grade students and nearly the same proportion, 32%, of other public school students were assessed at the Below Basic level in 2015.

NAEP Grade Four Reading: Percent Proficient		
Type of School	2003	2015
Public Schools (Non-Charter)	30%	32%
Charter Schools	26%	31%

Racial comparisons: Fourth Grade

Comparing public Charter school outcomes with other public school outcomes by race, we find that in 2003 12% of public Charter school Black students and 39% of White students were at the proficient or above level in fourth grade reading, as were a nearly identical 13% of Black students and 40% of White students in other public schools. In public Charter schools, 63% of Black students and 27% of White students at fourth grade were tested as Below Basic in reading, as were 61% of Black students in public schools and 26% of White students in public, non-Charter, schools. Similarly, by 2015, 17% of Black students and 44% of White students in Charter schools were at proficient or above, as were 18% of Black students and 46% of White students in public schools. Half, 49%, of Black students and 21% of White students in public Charter schools were at the Below Basic level in fourth grade reading, as were the same proportions of students in other public schools.

NAEP Grade Four Reading: Percent Proficient				
Type of School	2003		2015	
	Black	White	Black	White
Public Schools (Non-Charter)	13%	40%	18%	46%
Charter Schools	12%	39%	17%	46%

All Students: Eighth Grade

In 2005, 24% of public Charter school students scored at the proficient or above level in eighth grade reading, as compared to 29% of students in other public schools. 35% of the public Charter school students were classified as Below Basic in 2005, as were 29% of other students. In 2015, 31% of Charter school students were at or

216

above proficient, as were 33% of other public school students in eighth grade. A quarter of both public Charter school students and other public school students were Below Basic in reading at eighth grade in 2015.

NAEP Grade Eight Reading: Percent Proficient		
Type of School	2005	2015
Public Schools (Non-Charter)	29%	33%
Charter Schools	24%	31%

Racial Comparisons: Eighth Grade

Comparing Charter outcomes with other public school outcomes in eighth grade by race, we find that in 2005 9% of public Charter school Black students and 48% of public Charter school White students were at the proficient or above level in eighth grade reading, as were 11% of Black students and 37% of White students in other public schools. In public Charter schools, slightly more than half, 52%, of Black students and 19% of White students at eighth grade were below Basic in reading, as were 49% of Black students in other public schools and 19% of White students in public, non-Charter, schools. By 2015, 17% of Black students and 48% of White students in public Charter schools were at proficient or above in eighth grade reading, as were 15% of Black students and 42% of White students in other public schools. 39% of Black students and 12% of White students in public Charter schools were at the Below Basic level in eighth grade reading, as were 43% of Black students and 16% of White students in other public schools.

NAEP Grade Eight Reading: Percent Proficient				
	2005		2015	
Type of School	Black	White	Black	White
Public Schools (Non-Charter)	11%	37%	15%	42%
Charter Schools	9%	48%	17%	48%

All Students: Twelfth Grade

In 2009, nearly a quarter, 23%, of public Charter school students scored at the proficient or above level in twelfth grade reading, as compared to 37% of students in other public schools. 40% of the public Charter school students were classified as Below Basic in 2009, as were 27% of other students. In 2015, 21% of public Charter school students were at or above proficient, as were 36% of other public school students in twelfth grade. 45% of Charter school students and 29% of other public school students were tested as Below Basic in reading at twelfth grade in 2015.

NAEP Grade Twelve Reading: Percent Proficient		
Type of School	2009	2015
Public Schools (Non-Charter)	37%	36%
Charter Schools	23%	21%

Racial comparisons: Twelfth Grade

Comparing public Charter school outcomes with other public school outcomes in twelfth grade by race, we find that in 2009 just 11% of public Charter school Black students and more than three times that percentage, 36%, of White public Charter students were at the proficient or above level in reading. Higher percentages of each, 17% of Black students and 45% of White students, reached proficiency in other public schools. In public Charter schools nearly half, 46%, of Black students and 29% of White students at twelfth grade were Below Basic in reading, as were 44% of Black students in public schools and 20% of White students in public, non-Charter, schools. There was little change by 2015, when 12% of Black students and 46% of White students in public Charter schools were at proficient or above in twelfth grade reading, as were 16% of Black students and 44% of White students in other public schools. 58% of Black students and 21% of White students in public Charter schools were at the Below Basic level in twelfth grade reading, as were 48% of Black students and 22% of White students in other public schools.

NAEP Grade Twelve Reading: Percent Proficient				
Type of School	2009		2015	
	Black	White	Black	White
Public Schools (Non-Charter)	17%	24%	16%	44%
Charter Schools	11%	36%	12%	46%

Race and Income: Fourth Grade

Sorting by eligibility for the National Lunch Program within race, we find that there was little difference in 2003 in the percentages of Black students reading at grade level in fourth grade, either between those eligible for the program or those ineligible, between those in public Charter schools and those in other public schools. And there was also little difference in 2015 among eligible students, although ineligible students in non-Charter public schools did notably better than those in public Charter schools.

NAEP Grade Four Reading: Percent Proficient				
Black Students	2003		2015	
	Eligible	Ineligible	Eligible	Ineligible
Public Schools (Non-Charter)	9%	22%	14%	32%
Charter Schools	9%	19%	15%	27%

In 2003 White students who were enrolled in Charter schools at fourth grade did slightly worse than those in other public schools for both those eligible and those ineligible for the National Lunch Program. There was little difference between the groups in 2015, although among White ineligible students there was a small gap in favor of students in non-Charter public schools.

NAEP Grade Four Reading: Percent Proficient				
White Students	2003		2015	
	Eligible	Ineligible	Eligible	Ineligible
Public Schools (Non-Charter)	24%	45%	30%	54%
Charter Schools	21%	43%	31%	49%

In 2003 Black students eligible for the National Lunch Program who were enrolled in Charter schools at fourth grade tested at the Below Basic level 70% of the time. Eligible Black student who were enrolled in other public schools tested as Below Basic 66% of the time. Ineligible Black students in Charter schools were at the Below Basic level 49% of the time; those in other public schools did so 44% of the time. All in all, a slightly less worse showing for those in non-Charter public schools. In 2003 White students eligible for the National Lunch Program who were enrolled in charter schools at fourth grade tested at the Below Basic level 43% of the time. Eligible White student who were enrolled in other public schools tested as Below Basic 42% of the time. Ineligible White students in Charter schools were at the Below Basic level 22% of the time; those in other public schools did so 21% of the time.

In 2015 Black students eligible for the National Lunch Program who were enrolled in   public Charter schools at fourth grade tested at the Below Basic level 53% of the time. Eligible Black student who were enrolled in other public schools tested as Below Basic 52% of the time. Ineligible Black students in public Charter schools were at the Below Basic level 31% of the time; those in other public schools did so 33% of the time. In 2015 White students eligible for the National Lunch Program who were enrolled in public charter schools at fourth grade tested at the Below Basic level 32% of the time. Eligible White student who were enrolled in other public schools tested as Below Basic 33% of the time. Ineligible White students in Charter schools were at the Below Basic level 18% of the time; those in other public schools did so 14% of the time.

Race and Income: Eighth Grade

Sorting by eligibility for the National Lunch Program within race, we find that there was little difference in 2003 in the percentages of Black students reading at grade level in eighth grade among those eligible for the program between those in public Charter schools and those in other public schools. Among those ineligible for the program, there was some difference, favoring students in non-Charter public schools. This was reversed for eligible students in 2015, but continued to favor students in non-Charter public schools among ineligible students.

NAEP Grade Eighth Reading: Percent Proficient				
Black Students	**2005**		**2015**	
	Eligible	Ineligible	Eligible	Ineligible
Public Schools (Non-Charter)	8%	18%	11%	26%
Charter Schools	7%	13%	15%	23%

There was some difference in 2003 in the percentages of White students reading at grade level in eighth grade among those eligible for the program between those in public Charter schools and those in other public schools, favoring the latter. Among those ineligible for the program, the situation reversed, favoring students in Charter public schools. Among eligible White students in 2015 there was a considerable difference, favoring those in public Charter schools, but only a single point gap among students ineligible for the National Lunch Program.

NAEP Grade Eight Reading: Percent Proficient				
White Students	**2005**		**2015**	
	Eligible	Ineligible	Eligible	Ineligible
Public Schools (Non-Charter)	23%	42%	27%	50%
Charter Schools	19%	47%	36%	51%

In 2005 Black students eligible for the National Lunch Program who were enrolled in Charter schools at eighth grade tested at the Below Basic level 62% of the time. Eligible Black student who were enrolled in other public schools tested as Below Basic less often, 54% of the time. Ineligible Black students in public Charter schools were at the Below Basic level 41% of the time; those in other public schools did so slightly less often, 38% of the time. In 2005 White students eligible for the National Lunch Program who were enrolled in public Charter schools at eighth grade tested at the Below Basic level 30% of the time. Eligible White student who were enrolled in other public schools tested as Below Basic at about the same rate: 31% of the time. Ineligible White students in public Charter schools were at the Below Basic level 15% of the time; those in other public schools did so a virtually identical 16% of the time.

In 2015 Black students eligible for the National Lunch Program who were enrolled in Charter schools at eighth grade tested at the Below Basic level 41% of the time. Eligible Black student who were enrolled in other public schools tested as Below Basic more often, 47% of the time. Ineligible Black students in public Charter schools were at the Below Basic level 30% of the time; those in other public schools 28% of the time. In 2015 White students eligible for the National Lunch Program who were enrolled in public Charter schools at eighth grade tested at the Below Basic level 18% of the time. Eligible White student who were enrolled in other public schools tested as Below Basic, more often: 26% of the time. Ineligible White students in Charter schools were at the Below Basic level 10% of the time; those in other public schools did so a virtually identical 11% of the time.

Race and Income: Twelfth Grade

Twelfth grade results for Charter schools by race and National Lunch Program eligibility are only available for 2009, 2013 and 2015, and not for each group for each of those years. Ineligible Black students in public Charter schools were not reported in 2013 or 2015.

In 2015 Black students eligible for the National Lunch Program who were enrolled in public Charter schools at twelfth grade tested at the proficient or above levels 10% of the time (up from 7% in 2009). Eligible Black student who were enrolled in other public schools tested at the proficient or above levels 13% of the time (up from 8% in 2009). Ineligible Black students in public Charter schools were not reported in 2013 or 2015; those in other public schools were at or above proficient in 2015 24% of the time.

In 2013 White students eligible for the National Lunch Program who were enrolled in public Charter schools at twelfth grade tested at the proficient and above level 23% of the time. Eligible White student who were enrolled in other public schools tested at grade level and above 31% of the time in 2013 and 30% in 2015. Ineligible

White students in public Charter schools were at the proficient or above level 51% of the time; those in other public schools did so 48% of the time in 2015.

In 2015 Black students eligible for the National Lunch Program who were enrolled in Charter schools at twelfth grade tested at the Below Basic level 59% of the time (up from 48% in 2009). Eligible Black students who were enrolled in other public schools tested as Below Basic 53% of the time (also up from 48% in 2009). Ineligible Black students in public Charter schools were not reported in 2013 or 2015; those in other public schools were Below Basic in 2015 37% of the time. In 2013 White students eligible for the National Lunch Program who were enrolled in Charter schools at twelfth grade tested at the Below Basic level 41% of the time. Eligible White student who were enrolled in other public schools tested as Below Basic 28% of the time in 2013 and 30% in 2015. Ineligible White students in public Charter schools were at the Below Basic level 20% of the time; those in other public schools did so 19% of the time.

Subject Area Achievement Comparisons

There are complete NAEP U.S. History assessment results for eighth grade for public Charter school enrollment by race and income only for 2014. In that year, just 2% of Black students who were enrolled in public Charter schools and were eligible for the National Lunch Program reached the level of proficient or above. There were no results for Black public Charter schools students ineligible for the National Lunch Program. Eligible Black students in other public schools reached proficient and above just 3% of the time. 13% of those not eligible and not in a public Charter school attained the level of proficient or above. Among White students, there were no reported results for those eligible for the National Lunch Program and enrolled in public Charter schools. Among those ineligible, 35% in public Charter schools reached the level of proficient or above. Eligible White students in other public schools attained the proficient or above level 11% of the time, those not eligible did so 29% of the time.

There are complete NAEP Science assessment results for eighth grade for public Charter school enrollment by race and income only

Three-Fifths of an Education

for 2009, 2011, and 2015. In 2015, 8% of Black students who were enrolled in public Charter schools and were eligible for the National Lunch Program reached the level of proficient or above, as did 21% of Black Charter schools students not eligible for the National Lunch Program. Eligible Black students in other public schools reached proficient and above 8% of the time as did 23% of Black students in those schools not eligible for the National Lunch Program. Among White students, 28% of those eligible for the National Lunch Program and enrolled in public Charter schools reached the proficient or above level. Among those not eligible, 54% in public Charter schools reached the level of proficient or above. Eligible White students in other public schools attained the proficient or above level 30% of the time, those not eligible did so 54% of the time.

Conclusion

In general, there is little difference between the percentages of students brought to grade level in public non-Charter and public Charter schools. Comparing outcomes for all Black and White students, the records of Charter and non-Charter public schools are similar for Black students. White students are brought to proficiency in grade eight reading rather more often in public Charter schools than in other public schools. Both Black and White students from lower-income families reach proficiency in grade eight reading more often in Charter than in non-Charter public schools, while Black students from middle class families do rather better in non-Charter public schools than in Charter schools. The record of Charter schools in regard to Black students from lower-income families appears to be strongly influenced by that of the Charter schools in the state of George, where 33% of NLP-eligible Black students reach proficiency in reading in grade 8. The next highest percentage of NLP-eligible Black students reaching proficiency in reading in grade 8 is that for Illinois, at 14%.

Index

D

Dallas, Texas, 136, 137, 140, 141, 142, 213
Department of Defense, 15, 16, 18, 19, 20, 61, 65, 77
Detroit, 6, 52, 53, 54, 55, 78, 80, 81, 213
Doctorates, 48
Du Bois, W. E. B., 5, 10
Duke University, 101, 111, 118
Durham County, 111, 113
Duval County, 52, 53, 54, 55, 128, 129, 130, 131, 132, 133, 213
Duval County, Florida, 52, 53, 54, 55, 128, 129, 132, 213

E

Education Law Center, 182
educational attainment, 9, 13, 15, 31, 66, 67, 69, 85, 86, 92, 96, 99, 116, 127, 129, 132, 141, 142, 148, 150, 151, 157, 158, 161, 162, 165, 167, 171, 179, 199
educational opportunities, 15, 20, 25, 26, 27, 28, 29, 41, 47, 57, 58, 65, 73, 77, 78, 79, 81, 82, 83, 87, 102, 106, 107, 108, 113, 114, 117, 118, 122, 123, 124, 130, 133, 150, 155, 181, 182, 186, 191, 192, 193, 194, 197, 199, 200, 203, 205
Equity and Adequacy in Alabama Schools and Districts, 95
Evanston, Illinois, 173, 174
expenditure on instruction, 118

F

Fairfax County, Virginia, 121, 122, 123
family income, 7, 13, 19, 21, 26, 27, 28, 29, 57, 58, 67, 78, 80, 82, 87, 91, 94, 99, 105, 106, 116, 117, 120, 121, 122, 127, 135, 142, 145, 154, 161, 172, 179, 199, 203, 205
federal funding, 94, 122
Flint, Michigan, 78, 80, 83
Florida, 52, 74, 127, 128, 129, 130, 131, 132, 133, 135, 145
Founders, 7, 21, 86
functionally illiterate, 77, 80, 86, 92, 99, 106, 109, 141, 146, 148, 152, 158, 162, 167, 169, 171, 172, 180, 184, 194, 198, 200, 204

G

Georgia, 69, 74, 85, 86, 87, 88, 89, 90, 91, 93, 97, 103, 128, 133
Gilliam, Walter S., 39
Graham County, 113
Great Migration, 6, 66, 77, 165, 189, 197

H

Halifax County, 113
high school graduation rates, 49, 90
Hilliard, Ohio, 194, 195
Hillsborough County, 128, 130, 132
Hillsborough County, Florida, 128, 130, 131, 132, 133, 213
Hispanic-Americans, 7
Houston, Texas, 135, 136, 137, 138, 139, 140, 141, 142, 213

I

Illinois, 6, 75, 165, 166, 167, 168, 169, 170, 171, 174, 224
immigrants, 7, 10, 127, 133, 135, 145
incarceration, 60, 66, 96, 102, 103, 173
incarceration rates, 60, 102

227

Index of Dissimilarity, 97, 122, 147, 190

India, 24

Irish, 7

Italians, 7

J

Jackson, Mississippi, vii, 81

Jefferson, President Thomas, 24, 213

Jews, 7, 24

Jim Crow, 5, 10, 40, 66, 69, 73, 105, 111, 119, 122, 124, 127, 165, 181, 189, 197

Justice Center of the Council of State Governments, 43

L

Lake Erie, 189

Liberty City, 131

local funding, 122

Long Island, 181

Los Angeles, 147, 148, 213

Louisiana, 9, 40, 66, 67, 68, 69, 74, 94, 97, 98, 99, 100, 101, 102, 103, 135, 163

Louisville, Kentucky, 6

M

Maryland, 73, 74, 151, 157, 158, 159, 161, 163, 164

Memphis, 52, 81, 151, 153, 155

Mexico, 128, 135

Miami-Dade, 128, 131, 213

Michigan, 6, 9, 75, 77, 78, 79, 80, 81, 82, 83, 85

military families, 15, 19

Milwaukee, 6, 52, 54, 55, 213

Mississippi, 6, 9, 66, 67, 68, 69, 74, 75, 77, 78, 79, 81, 82, 83, 85, 94

Mississippi Delta, 151

Myrdal, Gunnar, 21

N

NAEP (National Assessment of Educational Progress), 16, 19, 21, 22, 23, 24, 25, 26, 28, 29, 30, 33, 34, 37, 45, 46, 49, 50, 51, 52, 53, 58, 68, 73, 80, 81, 92, 98, 99, 102, 114, 116, 119, 120, 121, 122, 137, 138, 140, 141, 147, 148, 149, 152, 153, 162, 163, 168, 169, 171, 174, 177, 178, 180, 184, 185, 200, 215, 216, 217, 218, 219, 221, 223

Nashville, 153

National Assessment of Educational Progress (NAEP), 16

National Bureau of Economic Research, 101, 182

National Center for Education Statistics, vii, 35, 51, 61, 62, 63, 207, 208, 209, 210

National Institute for Early Education Research, 105, 112, 120, 128, 136, 146, 166, 190, 198

National Lunch Program, 19, 21, 22, 26, 27, 29, 34, 37, 57, 58, 67, 68, 69, 79, 81, 86, 87, 89, 92, 98, 99, 112, 113, 114, 116, 120, 121, 129, 131, 132, 137, 138, 141, 146, 148, 152, 158, 159, 162, 163, 164, 167, 168, 171, 172, 177, 179, 185, 189, 191, 199, 204, 219, 220, 221, 222, 223, 224

New Jersey, 6, 75, 94, 103, 177, 178, 179, 180, 181, 182, 183

New Mexico, 7

New Orleans, 67, 97

New York, iii, 6, 9, 41, 43, 50, 52, 55, 75, 150, 163, 177, 178, 179, 180, 181, 182, 183

New York City, 6, 42, 43, 49, 50,
    51, 52, 66, 178, 179, 181, 184,
    185, 186, 213
New York Times, 182
NICHE website, 177, 178
North Carolina, 74, 111, 112, 113,
    114, 115, 117, 118
North Carolina State University, 111

O

OCR (U.S. Department of Education
    Office for Civil Rights), 39, 40,
    45, 46
Office for Civil Rights, 39, 45, 61,
    62, 93, 99, 107, 115, 117, 123,
    148
Ohio, 6, 9, 75, 189, 190, 191, 193,
    194, 195
Organization for Economic Co-
    operation and Development
    (OECD), 33
out-of-school suspension, 41, 42, 79,
    89, 93, 99, 107, 115, 117, 123,
    130, 132, 139, 141, 147, 148,
    154, 159, 163, 168, 173, 186,
    191, 201

P

paddling and spanking, 99
parental education, 30, 31, 58, 138,
    147, 150, 180, 205
Pathak, Parag A., 101, 102
Pennsylvania, 6, 9, 75, 197, 198,
    199, 200, 201, 206
Philadelphia, 6, 41, 42, 43, 49, 50,
    51, 52, 55, 198, 201, 203, 204,
    205, 213
Pinellas County, 133
Pittsburgh, 201, 205
poverty rate, 7, 67, 69, 82, 83, 86,
    111, 145, 157, 165, 189, 197,
    203

prekindergarten, 15, 70, 88, 97,
    105, 106, 112, 128, 129, 136,
    137, 143, 145, 166, 190, 197,
    198
Prince Edward County, 121, 122,
    123
private school, 82, 91, 100, 101, 108
Program for International Student
    Assessment (PISA), 33
pupil/teacher ratio, 173

R

racial discrimination, 5, 10, 11
racial gaps, 113
racial penalty, the, 8, 58, 59, 67
racial prejudice, 10, 58, 154, 172,
    191
racism, 5, 6, 10, 11, 25, 87, 111,
    174, 186, 187
Research Triangle, 111, 114
Richmond, Virginia, 121, 122, 123,
    124
rural schools, 88, 153

S

Saginaw, Michigan, 78
San Diego, 146, 147
San Francisco, 147
SAT, 46, 62, 90, 108, 115, 124,
    130, 139, 150, 160, 164, 194,
    201
school discipline, 39, 40, 41, 42, 43,
    93, 99, 107, 114, 117, 123, 139,
    142, 148, 172, 181, 200
school finance, 95
segregated schools, 78, 109, 133
Shelby County, Tennessee, 153
slavery, 5, 12, 69, 73, 88, 105, 121,
    123, 124, 197
socio-economic mobility, 9, 60, 86
Somerset County, Maryland, 157